CORPORATE COUNSEL GUIDES

Understanding Asia

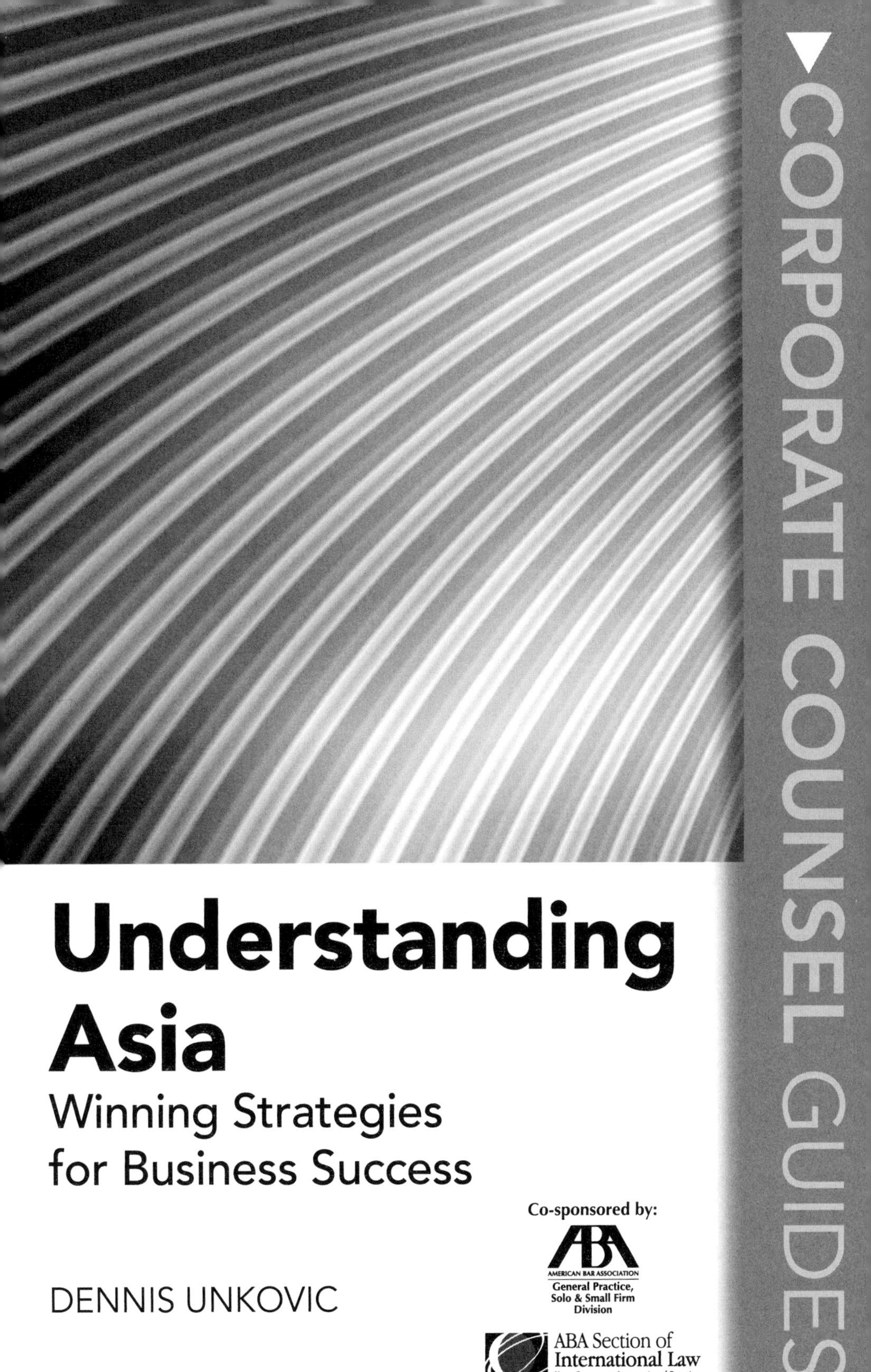
CORPORATE COUNSEL GUIDES
Understanding
Asia
Winning Strategies
for Business Success
DENNIS UNKOVIC
Co-sponsored by:
ABA
AMERICAN BAR ASSOCIATION
General Practice,
Solo & Small Firm
Division
ABA Section of
International Law
Your Gateway to International Practice

Cover design by Jill Tedhams/ABA Publishing.

Printed in the United States of America.

15 14 13 12 11 5 4 3 2 1

Library of Congress Cataloging-in-Publication Data

Unkovic, Dennis, 1948–
Corporate counsel guides : understanding Asia / by Dennis Unkovic.
p. cm.
Includes index.
ISBN: 978-1-61632-805-4
1. Business law—Asia. 2. Business enterprises—Law and legislation—Asia. 3. Corporate culture—Asia. 4. Business etiquette—Asia. I. Title.

KNC84.B87U55 2011
346.507—dc22

2010050178

Discounts are available for books ordered in bulk. Special consideration is given to state bars, CLE programs, and other bar-related organizations. Inquire at Book Publishing, ABA Publishing, American Bar Association, 321 North Clark Street, Chicago, Illinois 60654-7598.

www.ababooks.org

This book is dedicated to Bob Markel.
Thank you for your friendshp and wonderful guidance over so many years.

June 27, 2011

To Perry,

It has been great getting to know you and work together over the last year. I would be delighted if you will accept this copy of my book "Understanding Asia". Hopefully I got at least part of it right!

All the best

[illegible]

CONTENTS

AUTHOR'S NOTE

After 25 years spent traveling to Asia, there are too many individuals who influenced this book to thank here. I deeply appreciate the advice, warnings, counsel, and direction I have received throughout my career from business-people, lawyers, and personal friends throughout Asia.

A special note of gratitude goes to Heng Kim Song, who has become a good friend over the years. Heng is one of the leading freelance editorial cartoonists in the world. Since 1984, his cartoons have appeared weekly in the largest Chinese language newspaper in Singapore, Lianhe Zaobao, *and they are reprinted regularly in major periodicals such as* The New York Times, Newsweek, *and* Asahi Shimbun. *Over lunch one day in Singapore, I asked if he would consider contributing some of his original cartoons to this book, and he graciously agreed. It is an honor to be able to include Heng's works here. Looking at the world through Heng's eyes will treat the reader to an exceptional view of Asia.*

Once again, my thanks to everyone for their valuable input and assistance. I can assure the reader that any mistakes in this book are solely mine.

CHAPTER ONE
THERE ARE NO ASIANS

My first trip to Asia was in 1985. After returning home, I believed I had gained great insights into the five countries I had visited. How naive I was. I came to realize over the following years how little I actually knew. I did, however, learn one important lesson that has stuck with me ever since, and that is to be humble. No one can or will ever know everything about Asia or any individual country in Asia. Accept the fact that the person sitting on the other side of the table is at least as smart as you are and is likely to know just as much, if not more, about any proposed transaction. You cannot finesse or manipulate a negotiation in Asia. Try it and you will be eaten alive. Your only hope is to be as prepared as possible. This means you will have to leave all preconceived notions about how business is conducted in the Far East at home. The fact that you are successful where you live has no bearing at all on how you will perform overseas.

If you remember just one thing after reading this book, remember that Asia is merely the name of the Earth's largest continent—there are no *Asians.* Because Asia is made up of the most diverse mixture of individuals and cultures anywhere on earth, the term *Asians* is misleading. *Asians* simply do not exist. Everyone who wishes to have any sort of dealings in that part of the world must recognize and appreciate the unique characteristics of each country in Asia which help to distinguish it from its neighbors.

One common trend, though, is clear—business is becoming increasingly interdependent and internationally driven. Few companies have the luxury of focusing exclusively on their domestic markets, regardless of where they are located, and no business hoping to prosper can afford to ignore competitors that operate internationally. Tyson Foods provides one example. When it was formed thirty years ago, Tyson was an American poultry business that sold exclusively within the U.S. market. Then one day China presented itself as an opportunity for Tyson's products. Seemingly overnight, Tyson went from having no business in China to more than $750 million in sales in 2010. Tyson's story is emblematic of how companies in order to grow, and in many cases survive, must expand internationally.

As the worldwide economic recession slowly winds down, new opportunities in Asia will present themselves, creating professional challenges for in-house legal counsel and private law firms when they are asked for practical and timely advice on doing business throughout Asia. The basic challenge for lawyers, which this book seeks to address, is recognizing how drastically business methods and laws vary among Asian countries. A joint venture structure that works well in one country can be disastrous in another. Negotiating techniques are culturally driven and must be specifically tailored to each country. The degree of government involvement in regulating business, tax implications, social expectations, staffing questions, dispute resolution, and so forth must be addressed separately for each country. Unless legal counsel are attuned to these wide variances among the countries of Asia and prepared to advise clients appropriately, chances for a successful venture are slim.

The chapters of this book focus on specific Asian countries. The four most comprehensive chapters describe China, India, Japan, and Korea, which are currently the most dominant players in the region. Other chapters reveal the unique aspects of doing business in smaller but important economies such as Indonesia, Thailand, Singapore, Malaysia, and Taiwan. Finally, sometimes overlooked economies, but ones with a great deal of potential—such as Vietnam—are explored.

In short, this book provides in-house counsel and lawyers in private practice with practical advice on what to do and what not to do from country to country in Asia. While common themes such as negotiating techniques, use or avoidance of local court systems, and the scope of intellectual property protection appear in most chapters, the subject matter cannot justifiably be addressed in a compare-and-contrast format. Each chapter is distinctive as it attempts to present the intricacies, complexities, and unique aspects of doing business in the particular country addressed.

To be successful in the long run, business executives and lawyers must take the time to educate themselves, plan carefully, and prepare extensively. This book provides the first step on the journey.

CHAPTER TWO

CHINA AND INDIA: THE ELEPHANTS IN THE ROOM

Where does the sacred elephant walk?
Anywhere it desires.
—Indian Proverb

The face of Asia is fundamentally changing in ways that were not foreseen even ten years ago. Before examining the individual countries, I believe it is best to start by assessing current developments in Asia. There appear to be two emerging powers—China and India—which will collectively dictate what direction Asia will move in the future.

America in Asia: 1945 to 1990

When the Pacific phase of World War II ended with the Japanese surrender in Tokyo Bay, all of Asia lay in ruins. Even those countries that had "triumphed" basically had nothing. As a result, for the next thirty-five years American businesses paid little attention to Asia. Even as recently as the 1980s, the U.S. government looked at Asia more from a geopolitical and military than an economic perspective. This attitude came back to haunt America's prestige in Asia in the following years.

Underlying America's indifference was what I view as either ignorance or arrogance toward its Asian counterparts. Prior to the 1990s, most American industries expressed little concern for the head-to-head competition coming out of Asia. How naive America was to not see what was coming. First Japan, then Korea, and later the "Tigers" of Southeast Asia and Taiwan; one by one the countries throughout Asia began to emerge as increasingly competitive economic threats to American dominance.

If there is any excuse for America's overlooking the economic potential of Asia, one can argue it was America's involvement in the Vietnam War. Vietnam, which was viewed by Presidents Kennedy, Johnson, and Nixon as a direct challenge to America's military strategic position, consumed the attention of Americans, including the business community. By the time the Vietnam War ended, Japan was well on its way to becoming a world economic powerhouse. From 1986 to 1992, Japan entered what is known as its Bubble Period. During the Bubble Period, Japan appeared poised to surpass the United States as the world's largest economy by the end of the century. Unfortunately for Japan, the bubble burst, and by the early 1990s Japan fell into a decade of recession. Fortunately for the rest of the world, other Asian economies did not suffer a similar fate. In fact, except during the widespread 1997 Asian financial crisis, Asia as a whole continued to grow; Korea emerged as a major economic force, as did Taiwan and Singapore. More recently, countries like Indonesia and Vietnam have begun to surface as real players on the world stage.

A Slow Sunset in Japan?

Japan today is the third largest economy in the world (China surpassed Japan and took the No. 2 spot to the United States in August 2010). The challenge now facing Japan is that it has reached a peak in its growth cycle as a result of several factors. First, Japan is an aging society with a birthrate so low that it no longer replaces itself on an annual basis. Japan has come to be known as the World's

Greyest Society. In coming years, Japan will need to extract tremendous resources out of its national wealth to pay for the needs of its elderly who are no longer working and will have increased health care needs. Another factor influencing Japan's stagnation is its relatively small geographic size compared to other countries in Asia. With about half the population of the United States, Japan finds itself competing with major players such as China and India, both of which have growing economies and much larger populations.

The Elephants in the Room: India and China

With all due respect to Japan, it is India and China that will define Asia in the 21st century. Even after being displaced as the world's second-largest economy by China in 2010, Japan unquestionably will remain a strong economic power. Most economists project that China will ultimately surpass the U.S. economy in size within the next fifteen years.

Is it an accident that China and India have grown so quickly? Definitely not. Looking at China and India in 1980, both had approximately the same size economies with large populations living in poor, technologically backward conditions. Who could have guessed thirty years ago that China and India were destined to dominate the world's economy? Few experts back then predicted it. How each country went about transforming itself is an interesting story.

China's Plan

Since its Revolution, China has had a centrally controlled economy, but thirty years ago China decided to radically change course. The central government decreed that Chinese entrepreneurs would be permitted economic freedom, with the caveat that individual political freedom would not necessarily follow suit. The reason for this new philosophy espoused by Deng Xiaoping was China's realization that it needed to attract massive amounts of foreign direct investment. In

order to accomplish this goal, Chinese leaders began a sustained effort to build a world-class infrastructure.
Beginning with Special Economic Zones such as the Pearl River Delta in the South, and later with other carefully targeted efforts throughout China, the Chinese government pulled out all the stops to attract foreign-based manufacturing into China. The Chinese spent billions of dollars constructing ports, bridges, roads, railroads, and a power grid in order to provide the key resources every manufacturer needs to succeed. With new industrial parks and special areas targeted for investment, China has boomed in a way no other country has since America in the late 19th century during the height of the Industrial Revolution. China's approach to growth was to build infrastructure and supply low-cost, efficient labor pools.

It is hard to argue with the success of this plan—China has experienced anywhere between 8% and 12% annual growth over the last thirty years. To put it into perspective, if an economy grows at 8.5% per year, over a period of eight years, it doubles. You can see how many times the Chinese economy has doubled, and then doubled again, since the 1980s.

The Indian Path

India was far slower off the mark than China. Since gaining its independence, India has exhibited a deep-seated aversion to foreign direct investment. Part of this attitude is due to remnants of strong anticolonialism feelings, which is understandable following the many generations of British colonial rule the nation endured. Once India finally achieved its independence, the Indians believed they would do things their way with no need to involve outsiders. It was essentially "India for Indians."

From the 1950s through the early 1990s, India followed an NIH philosophy—that is, "not invented here." India's bureaucracy strongly opposed foreign direct investment or the licensing of technology that Indians had to pay for. The Indians continued to believe that they could develop whatever they needed themselves.

The results are better described in the chapter of this book focusing on India, but basically in the 1970s and 1980s India grew extremely slowly (i.e., about 3% a year as opposed to China's growth, which was three or four times as high). In the early 1990s, though, the Indians began to realize they had to change their way of doing business or else they would continue to lag behind China, Korea, and Japan. Over the last fifteen years, India has become much more open to foreign direct investment and is now growing at between 5% and 7% per year.

The Chinese Are Here; The Indians Are Coming

When thinking about Asia from 30,000 feet, the one thing to remember is that while Japan remains its second largest economy, Asia's future lies in India and China.

CHAPTER THREE

JAPAN: A NATION OF CONTRASTS

Japan's Imperial Palace sits in the center of Tokyo, an oasis of green amidst one of the most densely populated cities on earth. While thousands of people walk and jog around the palace's 5-kilometer perimeter each day, few have seen inside the high stone walls—it remains to this day the private residence of Japan's royal family. At the height of the Japanese real estate boom of the late 1980s, one expert calculated that the land directly under the palace grounds was worth more than all of the real estate in California. With scenic moats filled with exquisite multicolored carp and birds of all kinds, the Imperial Palace is serene and otherworldly. It is a symbol known throughout the world, reflecting a peaceful and nonaggressive image.

One mile north of the Imperial Palace sits the Yasukuni Shrine. Established in 1869, Yasukuni is a Shinto shrine devoted to the memory of 2.4 million individuals who served in the Japanese military. Among them are fourteen Class A war criminals who were convicted of crimes against humanity before and during World War II; they were enshrined at Yasukuni in 1978. Yasukuni signifies an ongoing debate within Japan. While Japan's militant period from the 1920s through the end of World War II is one that most Japanese would rather forget, its neighbors, particularly the Chinese and Koreans, will not. The Japanese themselves continue to debate whether honoring their controversial militaristic past is appropriate.

Each Japanese prime minister while in office must decide whether to make official visits to Yasukuni. Most other Asian countries believe it is a direct and personal insult if a Japanese prime minister visits the shrine. Interestingly, the late Emperor Hirohito on May 9, 1988, stated in a memo that it was a mistake to list the fourteen Class A war criminals among those to be honored for their World War II service. The current Emperor Akihito has not visited Yasukuni since he ascended to the throne in 1989.

The complex history of the Yasukuni Shrine provides just one example of the contrasts and contradictions in Japanese society. Japan is a country with vast diversity simmering just below the surface, and you can never assume that your first observation reflects reality.

During sixty trips to Japan over the past twenty-five years, I have had a front-row seat to Japan's roller coaster ride from booming prosperity in the early 1990s through its decade of decline to today's economic malaise. Japan in 2010 is the third-largest economy in the world after being surpassed by China in size in August 2010. China's ascension does not mean that Japan is failing, but this change does reflect how the power and economic structure of Asia is fundamentally changing.

Of any country in Asia, Japan maintains the closest political relationship with the United States. Mike Mansfield, the former U.S. Ambassador to Japan who also served as U.S. Senate Majority Leader during the 1970s, once described the relationship between Japan and the United States as the "single most important bilateral relationship in the world." In recent years, the relationship between the Japanese and American governments has become strained for a variety of reasons, but economic ties between Japanese and American companies have nevertheless remained strong.

Once again, Japan is a complex society, and failing to appreciate its unique nature will make any negotiation with the Japanese more challenging. This chapter outlines the nine key points any in-house counsel needs to recognize in order to successfully conduct business with the Japanese and their multinational companies.

POINT ONE
THE *KEIRETSU:* THE ROOTS OF CORPORATE JAPAN

To gain an understanding of how corporate Japan really works, you need to go back several hundred years. In the 18th and 19th centuries, the Japanese formed economic trading groups known as the *zaibatsu*, which were precursors to the vertically integrated corporations that emerged in the West in the late 19th century. The *zaibatsu* exercised great control over Japan both before and after the Japanese economy was forced to open up to the world by the unexpected arrival of Admiral Perry and his "Black Ships" in 1853. For two and a half centuries before 1853, Japan had existed in self-imposed isolation from the outside world.

During the Meiji Restoration beginning in the 1860s, Japan transformed itself into an industrial economy that slowly engaged in trade outside Japan. The *zaibatsu* groups were immensely powerful both economically and politically throughout the 1920s and 1930s. The word *zaibatsu* is no longer used in Japan, because the *zaibatsu* formed the backbone of the aggressive military industrial complex that led Japan first into invading China in the 1930s and then to attacking Pearl Harbor in 1941.

Following Japan's defeat in World War II, U.S. General Douglas MacArthur was placed in charge of the occupation of Japan from 1945 to 1951. MacArthur's first order of business was to dissolve the *zaibatsu* to punish those industrial groups for the role they played in nurturing the militaristic country of the 1930s. Nevertheless, as Japan slowly began to rebuild itself in the postwar era, basically the same *zaibatsu* groups were reconstituted, this time becoming known as the *keiretsu*. By the mid-1980s, a dozen or so *keiretsu* groups controlled more than 50% of the Japanese economy. A model *keiretsu* is shown in the following diagram.

Model of a *Keiretsu* Group

Trading Company (coordinates international sale of products and services)		Bank (financial arm)	
|	|	|	|
Operating Companies	Operating Companies	Operating Companies	Operating Companies
/ | \	/ | \	/ | \	/ | \
Suppliers	Suppliers	Suppliers	Suppliers

Sumitomo, Mitsui, Mitsubishi, Fuyo, and Sanwa are examples of large *keiretsu* groups. Toyota is perhaps one of the best-known examples of a vertically integrated *keiretsu* with an international reach. Toyota designs automobiles, subcontracts parts manufacturing to carefully selected suppliers, assembles its motor vehicles, finances its needs, and runs a massive worldwide distribution network.

In a *keiretsu* group (which can be vertical or horizontal), you will expect to find one or more manufacturing companies that produce diverse products. Tied to a *keiretsu*'s manufacturing group of companies is a bank (or group of banks) that historically serves as the primary lender to the group members (though not exclusively). A *keiretsu* also traditionally includes a trading company that has the role of marketing and selling products of the *keiretsu* companies internationally. Prior to the 1980s, most Japanese companies that were globally active did not have experience in international marketing and sales. As a result, within each *keiretsu*, a captive trading company became responsible for selling products of the group members all over the world. In addition, it is important to note that while the glue that once held together a *keiretsu* group was an extensive and interlocking network of cross-shareholdings and loans, cross-shareholdings are far less common today than in the past.

Look at Mitsui as an example of the breadth of a *keiretsu*. Founded originally in the 17th century, Mitsui was one of the largest *zaibatsu* groups in pre-World War II Japan. After the war, the Mitsui *keirestsu* emerged. Today, parts of this major industrial enterprise include companies intimately involved in petrochemicals, shipbuilding, oil exploration, chemicals, recycling, mining, construction, and engineering. Although they are independent now, the

Suntory beverage group, Toyota Motors, and Toshiba were once part of Mitsui. Sony, which is also independent, is acknowledged to have close business activities with Mitsui companies. Its primary financial arm is the Sumitomo Mitsui Banking Corporation with its principal headquarters in Tokyo. While not all *keiretsus* are as powerful as they were in the past, they are still major players in the Japanese economy.

Advice for In-House Counsel

1. Carefully research in advance whether you are considering doing business with a Japanese company that is part of an established *keiretsu.*
2. If a *keiretsu* is involved, investigate all members to determine whether there are any potential conflicts with your business plan. Also be sure to research the *keiretsu*'s reputation within the Japanese community and abroad.
3. Determine which Japanese bank is a primary or important lender to your potential venture partner, and conduct the requisite due diligence.
4. Be sure to have a strict and enforceable nondisclosure agreement in place to prevent your proprietary information from being shared with other companies within the *keiretsu.*

POINT TWO

INSIGHTS INTO NEGOTIATING WITH THE JAPANESE

Simply put, Japan is important. Even though the Japanese economy has weakened since the 1990s, Japan remains a key destination for inbound investment. Also, Japanese companies have made and continue to make significant investments in other countries around the world. For example, the Toshiba Corporation bought a controlling interest in Westinghouse Nuclear several years ago, indirectly making Toshiba one of the two world leaders in the commercialization of nuclear power. Consequently, whether doing business with the Japanese domestically or internationally, negotiating with the Japanese is an important skill to nurture.

Significant cross-cultural differences separate the Japanese from Americans. While no one should claim to be an expert on negotiating with the Japanese (particularly a Westerner), there are general concepts that can help to predict their behavior. Some Japanese are often uncomfortable being part of a strategic alliance or a joint venture because they prefer a business arrangement in which they can exercise significant control. Others, like Toshiba in its nuclear investment in Westinghouse, thrive in such a setting. Although the following approaches are not scientific, they draw upon twenty-five years of personal experiences dealing with the Japanese and may provide basic guidance to in-house counsel.

To begin, accept the fact that the Japanese are excellent and highly skilled negotiators. Anyone who fails to appreciate this fact is destined to encounter problems. However, there are certain patterns that recur during negotiations with the Japanese that, if recognized, can be turned to your advantage. Before negotiating with the Japanese, there are three fundamental approaches that you should adopt.

Approach One: Be sure to have a clear understanding of the type and scope of the relationship you seek to establish with a Japanese partner *before* entering into negotiations. Consider whether you are seeking a joint venture or an acquisition of a business or a technology. *Advice*: Many businesspeople make a mistake when they push to sign a "quick and dirty" letter of intent with the Japanese early in the process. They think having a memorandum of understanding

(MOU) is important, but I disagree. In my experience, where feasible it is better to skip the letter of intent stage altogether and go directly to substantive negotiations. Failure to project a consistent message of what you expect to achieve in a negotiation threatens its success. A letter of intent (or an MOU) is usually more of a hindrance than an advantage.

Approach Two: Expect your Japanese counterpart to be extremely well prepared for all aspects of the negotiation. Any American company is best advised when preparing for negotiations with the Japanese to spend much more time in advance than is usual. You will find that the Japanese tend to elongate negotiations for a variety of reasons, one of which is to be sure all of their deal points are adequately discussed. Therefore, you cannot rush the process. *Advice*: Be prepared to commit all appropriate time and resources if you expect your negotiations to conclude successfully. Do not make the classic American mistake of trying to force a conclusion. You may get a quick solution, but to your own detriment. Patience is the key.

Approach Three: True success in negotiating with the Japanese is more likely when you are willing to project your interests beyond the mere commercial aspects of a deal. *Advice*: Whenever possible, look for opportunities to establish non-business ties to your Japanese partner if you expect long-term benefits to flow to transfer your company. Negotiations in Japan extend to after hours. Go with the flow.

The Pre-Negotiation Stage

The pre-negotiation stage prior to formal discussions is arguably the most critical stage in the process. Following three critical steps during the pre-negotiation stage will help to facilitate the substantive negotiations which follow.

Step One: It is absolutely critical to find out as much as possible about the Japanese company with which you will be negotiating. The more you can discover about your opponent in advance of actual negotiations, the better chance you have of reaching a successful conclusion. For example, is the Japanese company you are negotiating with a member of a recognized *keiretsu*? Does your potential Japanese partner currently deal exclusively through a particular trading company? Would this relationship create any problems or possible strains on the joint venture under consideration? As is true with American companies, Japanese companies vary by reputation and internal ethical standards. Back-checking will alert you to where you need to be more cautious. *Advice*: Consider hiring a specialized Japanese consulting firm that is capable of providing your company with a private analysis of the reputation and commercial practices of potential Japanese partners. If you anticipate a significant negotiation with technology and/or capital at risk, it is worth investing some money into checking out your potential partner. Do this before you agree to a sit-down negotiation.

Step Two: If negotiations will involve the transfer of your company's technology (particularly if it is non-patented), be extremely cautious. This advice applies not just to Japanese companies but also to negotiating with other non-U.S. companies overseas. If you are a technology-oriented American company, realize that no other country in the world provides the same type of protection for trade secrets and non-patented proprietary information as the United States. *Advice*: Require your potential Japanese partner during the pre-negotiation stage to sign a binding confidentiality agreement. This agreement is intended to protect the confidentiality of all technology (i.e., trade secrets and proprietary information) as well as financial and other information you will disclose during negotiations. The key is to protect such information from the risk of disclosure if your negotiations ultimately fail.

Step Three: Be sure to allocate more time for negotiations with the Japanese than you would with an American company; the process is always deliberative with the Japanese. *Advice*: Decide on a budget in terms of both money and time that you are willing to commit to the negotiation process. Know the parameters in advance so you can properly gauge your strategy for the negotiations.

Negotiation Stage

While there are an infinite number of approaches you might adopt when negotiating with the Japanese, consider the following major points.

A. Appoint the members of your negotiating team in advance. Be prepared to advise the Japanese about the identity of your team early on—this will encourage them to do the same.

B. Designate one person on your negotiating team who will have the primary authority to negotiate on your company's behalf with the Japanese. Consistently defer to that person throughout the entire negotiation process. As described later, this person will probably not be a lawyer. It is also helpful to reserve the right to refer certain issues to individuals who are not on the negotiating team. One technique is to explain that the leader of your negotiating team has the authority to opine on most issues, but certain concepts must be reviewed and approved by the company's board of directors or an executive committee. This caveat gives negotiators the ability to step away from a difficult topic and return to it at a later point.

C. Try to get the Japanese company to agree in advance as to the composition of its own negotiating team. Pre-selection can avoid problems and helps to shorten the negotiating process.

D. It is important to note that the executives of most Japanese companies located in America (whether they are American or Japanese nationals) may not possess the actual authority to bind their parent companies on significant issues. Those decisions are most often made in Tokyo, Osaka, or the home office, and this has important tactical implications for negotiating on a major deal. Try to determine in advance if this is the case in your negotiations. Should you come to the conclusion that all decisions will ultimately be made by top executives of the Japanese parent company, consider either switching the negotiations to Japan, where the appropriate principals can participate, or request that a high-level designee from Japan join the negotiating team, so someone with true authority is available to approve major points in your negotiations.

E. Do not ignore the social aspects of the negotiating process. Although it is not necessary to host formal banquets, as is commonly the case with the Chinese, you should still strive to foster personal, non-business relationships with the Japanese negotiators whenever time permits. Setting aside a day during the course of negotiations for a round of golf or sightseeing is always a good idea. It helps to break the ice and creates the proper atmosphere for enhanced understanding.
F. Finally, set a realistic time frame for negotiations. Negotiations of major transactions have a certain life and are difficult to shorten. In a significant transaction like a joint venture, I have found that it is impossible to reach a final agreement with the Japanese in less than three months. If you want to accelerate the negotiating process, though, your goal should be to keep your talks to three meetings. Following is one of my techniques to accelerate negotiations by keeping your talks to three meetings.

Initial Meeting: This is the time and place for each side to exchange views, concepts, and strategies. Both parties must agree in advance that *all* substantive ideas must be put on the table for discussion at this stage. If possible, circulate beforehand a list of general topics to be discussed at the meeting. Ask your Japanese counterpart to do this as early in the process as possible. As long as all ideas are introduced for evaluation, no resolution of issues should be expected at this point. At the conclusion of the first meeting, the negotiating parties should delegate to specialized teams for each side (which have already been established) those questions they want to have answered prior to the next meeting. For example, any engineering, technical, marketing, antitrust, accounting, or legal problems should be examined by the subgroups. It is helpful to give the teams a specific time frame, such as six weeks following the initial meeting, to resolve or at least define options to resolve perceived roadblocks.

Second Meeting: In advance of the second meeting, circulate among the parties a list of those comments, options, and/or recommendations produced by the specialized subgroups after the first meeting. It helps to have a rough draft of an agreement available at the beginning of the second meeting, so when issues are resolved they can immediately be incorporated into the draft agreement. As described earlier, avoid the temptation to draft a memorandum of understanding or letter of intent, which wastes more time than it is worth. Following this second meeting, prepare a final draft agreement for review by the parties at the third meeting.

Final Meeting: Make the final draft agreement available for review by both parties in advance of the third meeting. Then, at the meeting, each side must have someone physically present who has the authority to reach agreement on specific areas of dispute. If not, arrange to have the Japanese party communicate key changes to its home office. In addition, be sure to have available a Japanese and an English version of the contract. This detail avoids the need for a last-minute translation. The finalized agreement should be initialed at that point for later signature by the parties at a ceremonial signing. Agree in writing that only one version (English or Japanese) will be used in the event a dispute arises.

The Post-Negotiation Stage

A major error often committed by American companies is to assume that all matters are settled once they have signed an agreement with their new Japanese partner. In many other countries around the world, a contract is not necessarily an end in itself. The Japanese, however, view a contract as a functional document to follow closely once it is signed. To aid American companies faced with this situation, the following three suggestions can help sustain the relationship between the Japanese and American companies during the post-negotiation stage. Simply relying on the contract is not enough if you expect to maintain a working relationship with the Japanese over a longer period.

Suggestion One: Assign an employee from the American company to follow up with the Japanese company on the points and obligations set forth in the contract. If certain written reports or other specific actions by the American company are mandated under the contract, be sure they are carried out as expeditiously as possible. One way to do this is to have the "point person" in the American company be an individual at an appropriately senior level. This signifies to the Japanese the importance of the contact to the American company. Similarly, require the Japanese firm to designate an internal contact person with whom your company will deal. In the event any misunderstandings or concerns arise as the contract is administered, the contact person should be able to address or appropriately refer such concerns.

Suggestion Two: Wherever possible, all concerns or potential problems in the contract implementation stage should be put *in writing* and sent to the Japanese partner for resolution. Oral communications without written verification are a constant source of friction. Writing down simple requests or questions lessens the possibility of confusion as a result of language, business, or cultural differences. It is wise to recognize that the Japanese language by its very nature is not as technically precise as English.

Suggestion Three: Continue to develop a broader non-business relationship with your Japanese partner. It is advisable periodically (at least once a year) to arrange a meeting between high-level executives from both companies. The meeting should be conducted so it is part business, part social. Golf, for example, provides a wonderful opportunity for business and social interaction. Also, your Japanese partner may establish a tradition of exchanging gifts with you at the New Year and during "Golden Week." As described elsewhere in this chapter, there will always be an air of formality and politeness with your Japanese colleagues, but when attempting to establish a long-term relationship, do not ignore the need for developing a comfortable, enjoyable social interaction.

POINT THREE

LAWYERS AND LEGAL PROFESSIONALS IN JAPAN

Japan's legal system is very different from the legal system in the United States. Far fewer lawyers in Japan are formally licensed to practice law. Each year, 40,000 to 50,000 individuals sit for the bar exam in Japan, and only about 3% pass. While pressure is now being exerted on the Japanese bar examiners to admit more lawyers, the bar has so far strongly resisted. In the future I believe the percentage will rise (though not much). The average candidate who successfully passes the Japanese bar exam has already taken and failed the test five or six times. Some candidates can spend years trying to be admitted, and many simply give up in frustration. Passing the bar in Japan is truly an accomplishment.

The small number of lawyers (*bengoshi*) admitted to the Japanese bar have an earned prestige within Japanese society, which comes with the ability to charge commensurately. This means that when you look to hire Japanese counsel, you will find few bargains at its premier firms. Moreover, do not expect to negotiate down their fees.

There is a special law in Japan governing the conduct of foreign (non-Japanese) lawyers. There are two ways for a foreign lawyer to work in Japan. One is to work informally, and the other is to seek certification as a *gaiben*. A *gaiben* must be approved by a special committee set up by the Japan Federation of Bar Associations, and the application process can take months. If the foreign lawyer is approved (and much has to do with reciprocity), then the *gaiben* calls himself or herself an "Attorney at Law for [insert name of state]." *Gaiben* can be involved in arbitrations in Japan, but cannot go into the Japanese court system. Basically, a *gaiben* cannot give advice on Japanese legal matters and is limited to providing counsel on his or her home country's laws.

As a general rule, foreign law firms operating in Japan do so in collaboration with a Japanese law firm. Typically, foreign lawyers work for a joint venture or within an established Japanese firm solely as a foreign legal advisor.

Aside from the role of foreign (non-Japanese) lawyers, it is important to note that the actual number of lawyers officially admitted to the bar in Japan is deceptive because it understates those individuals with legal skills. There are many more legal professionals in Japan than just bar members. For example, there are tax agents (*zeirishi*), patent agents (*benrishi*), those who draft legal documents for administrative agencies (*gyosei shoshi*), and private legal drafters (*shiho shoshi*). Even more significant, most Japanese companies have in-house legal departments staffed by individuals who are "law graduates" of universities but who have not been actually admitted to the bar. In short, these law graduates are highly skilled and legally trained, and it is a serious mistake to underestimate their abilities.

The Appropriate Role for American Lawyers in Negotiations with the Japanese

It is my view that while American lawyers can play a valuable role in negotiations with the Japanese, American lawyers working in Japan should not conduct themselves in the same way they would in the United States. American lawyers should act more as background advisors than as lead negotiators when representing an American company in negotiations with a Japanese company. While American lawyers can sit at the negotiating table, a more tactful stance will in most cases put the Japanese at ease.

It is worth mentioning that there is one role a lawyer can perform on behalf of an American company that has great potential value. Specifically, you can use a lawyer (Japanese in most cases) to make inquiries prior to and during negotiations with the Japanese party. This intermediary role can continue throughout the negotiations in order to ascertain progress or problems. In complex transactions, I always recommend that an American company retain a Japanese lawyer who will comment from a legal standpoint on contract provisions prior to finalization.

Point Four

Intellectual Property Laws in Japan

Japan has come a long way since the 1960s, when the country had a reputation for producing poor-quality products and constantly putting intellectual property at risk. Japan is now one of a handful of countries in Asia where protecting intellectual property is a priority for both parties to a transaction. Japan has signed all of the major international treaties governing protection of intellectual property, including the Paris Convention, the Berne Convention, and the Agreement on Trade-Related Aspects of Intellectual Property Rights (TRIPS).

Intellectual property protection is now a priority for the Japanese because Japan, as an advanced economy with its own locally developed technologies, requires IP laws to protect itself from outsiders. In my opinion, the courts of Japan will generally enforce intellectual property disputes on an evenhanded basis. A few points of note regarding Japanese courts are that there are no juries in Japan, and as a result all issues of fact and law are decided by judges. Japanese law also prohibits the imposition of punitive damages.

In addition to protection for utility patents, design patents, trademarks, service marks, and copyrights, Japan has specific legislation governing the production of semiconductor circuits and plant varieties. Japan also has an Unfair Competition Prevention Act which applies to trade secrets. While trade secrets are not as well protected in Japan as in the United States, there is a greater level of protection for trade secrets in Japan than almost anywhere else in Asia.

Point Five

Basic Business Structures in Japan

Any foreign company interested in doing business in Japan will be happy to know that it is possible for a non-Japanese entity to set up a wholly owned corporate structure in Japan with few exceptions. Those areas where the Japanese government does restrict outside investment include proposed ownership of airlines, broadcasting companies, and telecommunications carriers. Besides these few exceptions, outside investment is usually approved by the Japanese government unless it violates Japan's Antimonopoly Act, which is comparable to U.S. antitrust laws.

When doing business in Japan, there are four basic corporate structures available to either domestic or foreign entities. The most popular form of organization is called the *kabushi-kaisha*, usually referred to as a KK. KK is a limited liability for-profit corporation. The KK structure is the most common choice of business entity used in Japan by both Japanese and foreign investors. Unlike in the United States, it is difficult to conduct business in Japan unless you have adequately capitalized your KK. Every KK must have at least one representative director, and governance of a KK occurs through a board of directors and statutory auditors. Like corporations in the United States, each KK holds an annual shareholders meeting, and the actions of the KK can be approved by written consent with the concurrence of those involved.

Aside from the KK, there are three other available corporate structures: the *goudou-kaisha*, the *goumei-kaisha*, and the *goushi-kaisha*. These forms of organization are rarely used except as special-purpose vehicles. For a more extensive explanation, you should consult directly with legal counsel in Japan.

Point Six

Contracts in Japan

Elsewhere in this chapter I suggest various strategies to consider when negotiating a deal with the Japanese. The result of every successful negotiation is a written contract. It is, however, important to understand that the view of a finalized contract in Japan differs from the conception in most Asian countries (except Singapore). Throughout much of Asia, a signed contract is not viewed as a firm document that is to be followed without question. Instead, it is common in Asia to look at a contract as a fluid document that is easily changed or challenged by the parties when unexpected circumstances arise.

Japan is different. While it is difficult to bring a negotiation with the Japanese to fruition, a contract once signed is generally adhered to and respected by the Japanese. Obviously, if there is a major problem the contract can be challenged, though I have seen numerous cases in which a Japanese company found itself at a disadvantage but still followed the provisions of the contract to the end.

As to dispute resolution, the Japanese generally have a deep suspicion about all court systems outside of Japan. This perception is particularly true as applied to the Japanese view of the U.S. judicial system and its reliance on juries. Consequently, you can expect the Japanese to strongly object if you try to transfer dispute resolution outside Japan and particularly to American courts. If you have a contract with the Japanese and try to have a dispute resolved outside of Japanese courts, the Japanese will always insist upon arbitration. The controlling law is Japan's Arbitration Act, which came into effect in 2004.

Point Seven

The Japanese Political System

Just as General Douglas MacArthur was ending America's occupation of Japan in the early 1950s, the Japanese adopted a new constitution and created their own version of democracy "Japanese style." While the Japanese Constitution was in many ways modeled after the Constitution of the United States, Japan's political system in the end is quite different from its American counterpart. The two-party system that has served America so well over the past two centuries never took hold in Japan.

For almost 50 years, the Liberal Democratic Party (LDP) had a stranglehold on Japanese politics. Except for a brief period when it was out of power, the LDP exercised total control over Japan's political system until 2009. The LDP is a key reason the Japanese political system has changed so little over the last half century. With the Japanese construction industry and wealthy farmers as principal financial contributors to the LDP, it had no real opposition. Those and other industrial sectors underwrote the campaigns of Japanese politicians. "Why change when you have control?" was the unspoken mantra of the LDP for decades.

Japan's economy under the LDP leadership grew rapidly from the 1970s until early 1992, and Japan was envied by other industrial economies like the United States. The period from 1986 to 1992 ultimately came to be known as Japan's Bubble Period, during which it seemed as though Japan could do no wrong. When Japan's bubble burst with a vengeance in the early 1990s, the Japanese economy went into a deep and sustained recession that lasted for more than a decade. Some observers believe that Japan has not yet recovered from the recession of the 1990s. Look at the Japanese Nikkei index (stocks), which plummeted from about 40,000 in the early 1990s to below 10,000, where it is now. In other words, a publicly traded stock in a Japanese company worth $100 in 1992 is only valued at $25 today.

The slow and persistent stagnation of Japan's economy has been a constant irritant to the Japanese people. Then, without much warning, the unexpected happened. In August 2009, the LDP was defeated by the opposition, the Democratic Party of Japan (DPJ). Yukio Hatoyama was elected prime minister of Japan in September 2009. Hatoyama ran for office on a platform of moving Japan away from the traditional path that had been promoted by the LDP. The election of Hatoyama resulted in political conflicts with the United States. Prime Minister Hatoyama did not last one year before he was replaced. Whether the DPJ will be successful in charting a new course for the Japanese economy is unclear, but this rapidly changing political landscape is an important trend that any company doing business in Japan must understand.

Point Eight

The Role of the Government in Japan

By the end of World War II, Japan's infrastructure and economy were completely destroyed. Then, in less than thirty years, Japan rebuilt itself into the second-strongest economy in the world, where it remained until August, 2010 when China surpassed Japan for second place to America..

This regeneration was not an accident. One fundamental reason for Japan's resurgence was the direct intervention by the Japanese government in prioritizing and allocating resources to certain industries. Back in the 1970s and 1980s, the Ministry of International Trade and Industry (MITI), which was a powerful bureaucracy in Japan, had the power to allocate loans to support certain industries needed to sustain the country's growth. Targeted intervention helped the Japanese economy to grow quickly. At first, loans and grants were directed to underwrite the emerging Japanese steel industry. This was followed by the Japanese automobile and electronics sectors and led to the rise of "Corporate Japan" throughout the 1980s. The rocket took off in earnest around 1986, and self-styled experts predicted that Japan would surpass the United States as the No. 1 economy in the world by the year 2000.

Unfortunately for Japan, when its bubble burst in the early 1990s, even the powerful MITI was unable to stop the downward spiral. MITI was renamed in 2001 and is now known as the Ministry of Economy, Trade and Industry (METI). While it no longer holds the kind of power that its predecessor did, METI today plays an essential role in directing Japan's economic development initiatives. Whether the successors to the Hatoyama administration will embrace the role of METI, assuming the DPJ retains a majority, is not yet clear.

Historically there has been a close (and some would say almost incestuous) relationship between MITI (now METI) and corporate Japan. The Japanese Business Federation (*Nippon Keidanren*) is the major trade organization that represents the interests of larger companies in Japan. With over 1,600 members and its main office in Tokyo, the Japanese Business Federation was formed by combining two organizations (*Keidanren* and *Nikkeiren*) that came into existence shortly after World War II. *Nippon Keidanren* is still very powerful and has a broad reach throughout corporate Japan and with the Japanese bureaucracy. It is useful to understand these dynamics if you are going to make a significant investment in Japan.

Point Nine

Ten Commonsense Tips Every Business Visitor Should Know about Japan

After visiting Japan for the first time and encountering many new experiences, you may be tempted to think you actually understand Japan. Resist this urge—you don't.

Over the years, I have discovered ten tips that will help any businessperson or lawyer to avoid missteps on their first, second, and twentieth visits to Japan.

1. *Business Cards.* Business cards in Japan are called *meishi*, and for the Japanese symbolize much more than a piece of paper. *Meishi* have a special and unique purpose in Japanese society and business circles. Your *meishi* does not merely spell out your name, title, and contact information; it is a reflection of who you are. Before your next trip to Japan, print your name in Japanese on the opposite side of your business card. Present it to those you meet with two hands, like a sort of offering. Equally important, remember that when meeting someone in Japan you have to pronounce your name clearly and correctly, and make certain your Japanese counterpart does the same. I can use my name "Unkovic" as an example. "Unko" when pronounced one way in Japanese means nothing, but by using a different inflection in Japanese "unko" means "shit." I know when someone is making a joke about me when I hear the wrong pronunciation. The lesson is to always clearly pronounce your name; otherwise, you might get an unpleasant surprise.
2. *Business vs. Casual Dress.* Business dress in the United States was once formal, but in recent years informality of dress has become the rule rather than the exception. This is not the case in Japan. Japanese businesspeople dress in a more formal

manner at all times, even during Japan's punishingly humid summers. If you are a man, always wear a suit and tie in Japan. A colored or striped shirt is fine, but flagrant informality is a way to get off on the wrong foot even in social circumstances. For women, the rules are a bit looser, but female executives should still err on the side of formality.

3. *Respect for Titles.* When meeting a Japanese business executive for the first time, take special note of his or her title. Japanese business cards and correspondence are always helpful because they list the title and exact position someone holds within a company. While Japan is a democracy, the concept of equality is not the same within its corporate culture. Japanese companies, especially the very large ones, are extremely hierarchical, and the title that a person holds is crucial. If you want to impress someone upon first meeting them, you might say, "Mr. Yamamoto" (or more appropriately, "Yamamoto-san"), "I see you are the second director of the Research and Development department of ABC Company. This is a very interesting and important position. Can you tell me what you do?" You can never go wrong in Japan by asking someone about their job and how important he or she is within the company's structure.
4. *Corporate Hierarchy.* In large Japanese companies, people rise within corporate ranks in different ways. Historically, a person's age has been more important than any other characteristic. While this "reverse age bias" is changing in Japan, never assume that someone who holds a title of general manager or an upper-level corporate position is there because he or she is the most competent person for the job. At the same time, larger Japanese companies are quite strict about forcing executives into retirement when they reach the age of sixty or sixty-five. The hierarchical structure requires an "up or out" approach so younger people can ascend to higher levels within the company.
5. *Bowing.* When you see two Japanese business executives greeting each other, in most cases they will bow instead of shaking hands. Bowing is the Japanese way. What you will observe is that the person holding a lower-level position will bow slightly

more deeply than the other who holds a higher position. It is a sign of respect. When two people are really not sure who is superior in rank, you will see them bowing again and again, each one trying to bow lower than the other. The joke is that they will eventually find themselves prostrate on the floor. What to do as a Westerner? In my experience, when first meeting a Japanese executive, do not greet in the automatic American or European way by sticking out your hand. Greet them, nod briefly, and allow them to take the first step. If they do not extend their hand to you, then simply do not extend yours; just bow slightly, and say, "It is a pleasure to meet you." Also remember the importance of knowing at least three phrases: *ohayo gozaimasu* ("good morning"), *konichiwa* ("good afternoon"), and *konban wa* ("good evening"). If you know those three phrases along with the term *domo arigato* ("thank you very much"), you will be far ahead of the pack.

6. *Gifting.* Much has been written about the ritual of giving gifts in Japan. Trust me, this is really not as important as you have been led to believe. While the Japanese exchange gifts among themselves for personal and cultural reasons, as a Westerner you are not really expected to participate. Japan is a wealthy and advanced society; so do not think you are doing someone a favor by handing them a pen with your company's name on it. Perhaps a pricier gold pen with a small symbol on it is fine, but inexpensive token corporate gifts are better left in your suitcase. When in doubt, do not gift. If you give a gift, be careful and think before you give something. For example, never give a Japanese contact a knife. The Japanese have a centuries-long history of producing the best knives in the world. Your letter opener worth $50 will make you look like an idiot. You can even offend a Japanese companion with how your gift is wrapped. For example, when there is a death in a Japanese family, it is common for a friend or associate to give the family a bereavement gift wrapped in white paper. Obviously, giving your Japanese business partner a gift wrapped in white paper would send the wrong impression. If you do wish to give a gift to a Japanese colleague, try to think

of something that is unique and cross-cultural. I often give individually handmade glass paperweights from an art center located near my home. They are beautiful, unbreakable, unique, and can be appreciated as either an art piece or a simple desk accessory.

7. *Personal Inquiries.* Americans are overly aggressive when talking about themselves, their families, their marital status, and particularly their children. When in Japan, avoid overly personal comments, and do not inquire about a Japanese executive's family. Do not even ask if the executive is married. If they want you to know, they will tell you. Along the same line, never expect to be invited to someone's home in Japan. The Japanese home is rarely, if ever, open to foreigners. There are a number of reasons for this, but the point to remember is that being invited to a restaurant is not an affront to you.
8. *Manners.* The Japanese are unerringly polite. It is culturally important that they appear open yet at the same time not intrusive. Speak softly and avoid using harsh words or obscenities in Japan. This point may sound obvious, but you would be amazed how often Westerners—knowingly or unknowingly—break this rule.
9. *Never Say No.* One aspect of Japanese business and culture is that the Japanese rarely, if ever, say no. If you find yourself in a negotiation and your Japanese counterpart says in response to one of your suggestions, "What you suggest may be difficult to accomplish," that statement is as close as you will ever come to an outright no. Listen for the signals, yet avoid confrontation. There is no benefit to embarrassing your Japanese counterpart. Moreover, if you tell your Japanese counterpart that something is a "deal breaker," you may find you have ruined a negotiation by creating a situation that forces the Japanese party to withdraw.
10. *The Two-Level Negotiation.* During business negotiations in Japan, there are often two negotiations going on simultaneously. One is the public negotiation in which the parties sit across the table from each other in a formal setting. The other is the subtle (yet equally important) negotiation going on in

the background. If you observe closely, you can identify on the Japanese negotiating team an individual who shuttles back and forth between the two sides passing on messages in an informal manner. An American company should also assign someone to take on the same role. This can be quite useful. If you anticipate a serious business point coming up in your negotiation to which you will need an answer, you can alert the Japanese side informally through this person regarding what is to come. That way the Japanese can ponder your suggestion in advance and not be confronted for the first time during open negotiations and be forced to respond. Embarrassing the Japanese is the worst thing you can do.

CHAPTER FOUR
INDIA: IS IT FOR REAL?

An American businessman traveled to India for the first time to set up a technology subsidiary in Bangalore. He engaged the services of a well-known international accounting and audit firm to assist with structural issues and tax planning. At one point, consideration was given to running the operation through a firm located in Mauritius for tax reasons, but eventually this option was discarded. At the end of the transaction, the bill arrived and included a $200 fee for reserving a name in Mauritius by purchasing an off-the-shelf shell company.

The businessman refused to pay this fee because he had never asked for the shell company to be formed and there was never a firm decision to go to Mauritius. The accounting partner persisted, however, arguing that buying the shell company was a prudent move that would have saved time had they elected to proceed in Mauritius. Furthermore, the accounting partner maintained that since the businessman's instructions were not precise, he did what he thought was appropriate to protect the businessman's interests.

Not having authorized the fee, the businessman demurred and simply refused to pay. At every meeting for the next three years and during the course of work totaling more than $25,000 in billings for tax, audit, accountancy, and consulting work, this small invoice was brought up and payment politely requested. The businessman became quite exasperated with the ceaseless requests and advised the local partner that he did not wish to hear of it again. The local partner agreed, and he was good to his word. However, the matter was passed on to Delhi, and the senior partners at the

Indian headquarters began making quarterly calls to the businessman requesting payment of the $200 fee.

The matter was finally resolved when the accounting firm was bidding on a new project for the same subsidiary and in the course of long, grinding negotiations finally agreed to make a modest price concession. "Ah," cried the businessman, "You don't need to give me the whole concession, just please credit $200 of it against this damn fee for the Mauritius firm." Great ceremony was given to documenting this negotiating point and—finally—the requests for payment ceased.

This anecdote highlights some of the particularities of doing business in India, where details are exacting, conversations are polite, negotiations are never-ending, and pursuit of payment is relentless.

For more than thirty years, India's progress was overshadowed by China's explosive economic growth and development. Only now is India beginning to emerge as a serious challenger to China in Asia, and this rivalry is likely to continue evolving over the next fifty years. Although it is home to 1.1 billion people and the world's largest democracy, India remains one of the world's least understood societies.

Without question, India will grow as an increasingly attractive destination for Western-based companies looking to expand in Asia throughout the next decade. Many economists now believe that India over the long term may offer foreign investors even more significant opportunities than China. As in-house legal counsel, you need to educate yourself on how best to do deals in India because its environment poses unique business challenges quite different from those encountered in China. This chapter contextualizes the challenges of doing business in India by providing an overview of the country's demographics, outlining strategies for foreign direct investment, and highlighting key contractual drafting concerns.

Overview of India—The Basics

Demographics

Although India is home to 17.5% of the world's population, many international businesspeople fail to comprehend the full implications of this statistic. Of the 1.1 billion people who are native to India, 63% of them are between the ages of 15 and 64. What is significant is that most of the population is at the lower end of the scale, making India a country with a very young population. In addition, although most of India remains predominantly rural, the country boasts more than twenty-five cities with populations in excess of 1 million people. As evidenced by its domestic income statistics, India finds itself in the midst of transforming from an agricultural society to a nation focused on urbanization and industrialization. Approximately 2% of Indians (about 20 million people) make up India's upper class, which registers a per capita income of more than $13,000.00 USD and provides a large and dynamic market of potential consumers for ambitious American and European exporters. Another 50 million Indians comprise India's burgeoning middle class. Arguably, India's middle class is larger than China's.

Economy

India's economy grew more than 6 percent in 2010, despite the world recession and the fact that the overregulation of business by the Indian government continued to restrict its ability to expand. Southern and Western India (including the populous cities of Mumbai, Chennai, Bangalore, Mysore, and Hyderabad) represents the geographic area in India where the most economic expansion is now taking place. It currently accounts for more than 50% of India's information technology production and research capacity. Experts expect this region to grow an additional 60% by the year 2020. Even during the economic downturn of 2009, the Indian economy outpaced most other economies in Asia (except for China).

Language

The official language of India is Hindi, but there are also twenty-three languages and 200 other dialects in daily use nationwide. Under the Official Languages Act of 1963, English may be used as a secondary language throughout India, and its use is especially widespread in the fields of commerce and business. Fluency in English is a major advantage for Indian businesses seeking foreign direct investment that cannot be matched by its Chinese competitors.

Religions

Eighty-three percent of the Indian population belongs to the Hindu religion. While there are numerous other religious sects throughout India, including Sikhs, Christians, Buddhists, and Jains, it is the Muslim population which makes up the second largest religious group by size (representing about 12% of the total population). Historically, most of the major religious conflicts have occurred in Northern India between the Muslims and Hindus.

Governmental Structure

Unlike the United States, India is a federation comprised of six centrally administered union territories and twenty-nine states. Each of the twenty-nine states and six union territories maintains its own separate capital to oversee local administration, and New Delhi is the capital where the union territories are administered.

India's Parliament

The Indian Parliament is composed of an upper house (Rajya Sabha) and a lower house (Lok Sabha). The Parliament is the country's highest legislative body, which operates in a manner similar to the British parliamentary model. Every five years, a major national election takes place for members of Parliament, unless there is a failure of support for the coalition government in power calling for an interim election.

Having provided a basic overview of India's cultural and political background, the following portion of this chapter outlines nine points that in-house legal counsel need to understand if asked to advise on possible projects or investments in India.

POINT ONE

FOREIGN DIRECT INVESTMENT IN INDIA: PAST, PRESENT, AND FUTURE PROSPECTS

Until about a decade ago, India had a poor record of attracting foreign investment. In fact, India's economic growth between 1980 and 2000 was about one-third of that which China experienced. One reason for India's limited growth during this period can be attributed to the fact that only 30% of its population resided in cities. The primary reason, however, is because of the past policies of its central government and bureaucrats who opposed what they viewed as "unwanted" foreign incursions into India's economy. Since India declared its independence in 1947, it has functioned as a highly regulated economy with a complex and multilayered bureaucracy making things happen—or not happen. Until relatively recently, the Indian government directly and indirectly held down foreign investment in a nationalistic effort to encourage domestic industrial concerns to grow and prosper without outside (foreign) competition. Unfortunately, these protectionist policies failed to stimulate the projected levels of domestic growth and ended up severely retarding the potential development of the Indian economy for decades.

One unforeseen consequence of India's slow economic growth between 1980 and 2000 came to be known as its "brain drain." Simply put, India's brightest young people left India to be educated at universities overseas, and most of those highly talented individuals never returned. Nevertheless, while the Indian government was discouraging foreign investment through ill-conceived government policies, at the same time it rightly took an important step by underwriting the costs of funding numerous world-class educational institutions throughout the country, such as the Indian Institute of Technology (IIT). These Indian institutions began producing top-notch graduates in a broad range of disciplines such as engineering, medicine, business, computer software and design, and the sciences. Unfortunately for those Indian graduates, few well-paying job opportunities were available in their native country. As a result, India suffered a secondary brain drain in which its top-level graduates left for other countries offering greater economic opportunities (the United States and high-tech companies in the Silicon Valley being the favored destinations). India's anemic growth of less than 4% between 1980 and 2000 was compounded by the loss of well-educated technical graduates. While some of India's brightest still leave for employment opportunities elsewhere, fortunately for India this brain drain has slowed in recent years. With the rapid acceleration of economic opportunities (particularly in Western and Southern India), large numbers of highly educated Indians are moving back home to take advantage of emerging opportunities. This trend is essential for India's long-term growth.

It is interesting to contrast how the Chinese government's top-down model for growth differed from India's. During this crucial twenty-year period, the Chinese government pursued a different strategy by aggressively seeking out foreign investors from the United States and Europe and creating the infrastructure that is essential to support world-class contract manufacturing export capabilities. This activity started in Southern China in the early 1980s and later spread to Shanghai, Fuzhou, Beijing, and selected cities in Central China. China's growth from 1980 to 2000 averaged a spectacular 9% to 10% (more than twice the rate in India). As a consequence, China's per capita income by the year 2000 was 70% higher than India's. This is a phenomenal statistic considering both countries were about the same in 1980.

As India found itself falling rapidly behind China, India's government became concerned and slowly began to alter its traditional opposition to foreign direct investment. With an exploding population, the Indian government belatedly acknowledged that a more vibrant economy funded by foreign investors was the only real key to sustained long-term growth. In July 1991, India trumpeted what came to be known as the New Industrial Policy Statement (NIPS). NIPS was the first of many steps intended to liberalize how foreign investment was viewed in India. In conjunction with NIPS, the Foreign Investment Promotional Board (FIPB) became the major center for regulating foreign investors seeking to gain a foothold in the Indian economy. Its efforts to liberalize India's historical aversion to foreign investment ultimately succeeded, and today India is one of the best regions in the world for foreign investors.

Because India is both a geographically and economically diverse country, the economic growth resulting from foreign direct investment has not evenly spread throughout India, and some regions have benefited much more than others. Western and Southern India provide the best examples of successful foreign investment to date. Key cities in these regions, such as Bangalore, Chennai, Hyderabad, and Mysore, are home to many of India's finest institutions of higher learning, and foreign investors can now benefit from the untapped reservoirs of highly educated individuals with in-demand IP and technical skills located in these areas.

India was one of the founding members of the General Agreement on Tariffs and Trade (GATT) in 1947. The World Trade

Organization (WTO), as the successor to GATT, is now tasked with further opening up global trade. The WTO is putting pressure on all countries including India to open their domestic markets to foreign competition and encourage outside investment. India has somewhat reluctantly gone along with this move toward liberalization, but the trend is clearly toward a more open framework.

This begs the question: *What are the prospects for future foreign direct investment in India?* The answer is, the prospects are very good. One reason for this optimistic outlook is that the Indian bureaucracy is now slowly beginning to dismantle the protectionist barriers it erected over the past few decades, which will create a more responsive environment for qualified foreign investors. Nevertheless, the Indian government remains much more restrictive than its Chinese counterpart with respect to allowing foreign direct investment. Although foreign direct investment is now permitted in India, Indian laws treat various economic sectors differently when it comes to outside investors. Some areas, such as the industrial sector, are favored for foreign investment while other areas, such as anything related to agriculture, face far more restrictions. For example, there are statutory restrictions under Indian law regulating how much capital a foreign investor can bring into India as well as the maximum percentage an outsider can own in certain types of Indian companies. In some areas, foreign investors are permitted to own up to 100% of the total share capital without governmental interference. This is called the automatic route. In those industries where foreign direct investment does not fall under the automatic route, advance permission from the Indian government is required before a foreign entity is allowed to make an investment. Moreover, the size of any outside investment (percentage of foreign ownership) is constrained by statute or regulations. For example, in the defense production industries or the insurance sector, the level of foreign investment is currently capped at 26%, despite pressure to raise this percentage. In addition, a foreign investor cannot own 50% of the equity in a domestic (Indian) air carrier.

To the extent that an overseas investor wants to own a business in India that falls in the field of agriculture, such companies must obtain general or special permission from the Reserve Bank of India. India continues to closely protect its agricultural sector from outside influences, and the ownership of agricultural companies in India remains highly politicized.

If a foreign investor does not elect to establish its own subsidiary or form a joint venture with an Indian partner, the investor has several other options. Specifically, an investor in India can look to establish a branch office, a project office, or a liaison office. Approval of the Reserve Bank of India is normally required for opening such offices.

A. A *liaison office* (also known as a representative office) is often set up by foreign companies that wish to oversee their existing business interests in India. It is important to understand that a representative office in India cannot itself undertake any direct commercial activity. If no revenue is generated by a liaison office, no significant tax implications exist for a foreign company in India. At the same time, a foreign company with a representative office in India has to be quite careful because it cannot repatriate money out of India.

B. A *branch office* is not an incorporated company but an extension of a foreign company doing business in India. Its activities are limited by Indian law and regulations, which specifically govern what a branch office can and cannot do. Like the liaison office structure, a branch office may undertake only a limited range of activities.

C. A *project office* is most often set up by a foreign company to carry out projects in India that have been awarded to the parent company. A project office works on government-funded projects on a limited basis. When a specific project is completed, its corresponding office is typically closed.

The Joint Venture

Under the Indian Companies Act, it is now possible to set up a joint venture between an Indian company and a foreign investor. Before 2005, the Indian government placed restraints on joint ventures between Indian and foreign companies. In January 2005, in an abrupt turnaround, the FIPB removed most of the former restrictions. Joint ventures today are encouraged, particularly for technology-based industries that offer to bring emerging technologies and research and development capabilities into India from abroad.

The joint venture is now a popular vehicle for foreign companies. If a foreign entity owns less than 51%, the parties can expect to receive automatic approval from the Reserve Bank of India. On the other hand, for those joint ventures in which a foreign entity has majority ownership or equity interests, approval may depend on the type of business involved. For example, the Indian government gives favorable treatment to certain industries (thirty-five currently) such as drugs and pharmaceuticals, electrical equipment, fertilizers, and biotechnology, because India is seeking investment in these areas. In short, in-house counsel should carefully review these statutes and regulations to determine what level of investment is permitted before making any firm commitment to proceed with a joint venture in India.

The Subsidiary

Another alternative for doing business in India as a foreign company is to set up a subsidiary. However, there are restrictions that foreign investors need to analyze in order to decide whether establishing a subsidiary is the best option. One hundred percent foreign ownership is now permitted in the sectors of hotel and tourism, real estate development, and parts of the pharmaceutical industry. Foreign investors will generally find that wholly owned operating subsidiaries are a possibility in most industries, but this should be carefully evaluated in advance before making any firm commitments in India.

While India has experienced sustained and significant foreign investment in its Central and Southern regions, fondly known as India's Silicon Valley, significant foreign investment has lagged elsewhere in the country. In the long run, one can anticipate that increased opportunities for foreign investors in other regions of India will emerge.

POINT TWO

INTELLECTUAL PROPERTY IN INDIA

For decades, adequately protecting intellectual property in India was a major issue for outsiders. On a macro level, India has a broad range of laws covering intellectual property, including the Indian Patent Act that goes back to 1970 and a recently updated trademark law. There are also specific acts covering the protection of designs, semiconductor circuits, general copyright issues, and plan varieties. Despite the existence of these laws, a challenge remains with enforcement. With the advent of an activist WTO and a growing desire within the Indian government to attract quality foreign investment, India's protection of foreign intellectual property has slowly improved.

From my experience, the area offering the greatest protection for foreigners today is trademarks. Notably, India has recently passed a new trademark law that broadened coverage in a number of key areas. Specifically, the trademark law provides for a ten-year term for trademarks, instead of the prior seven-year term. India has also announced that it is now prepared to review the concept of registered service marks, collective marks, and "well known" marks. The Indians assert that well-known marks are entitled to higher levels of protection because they are more likely to be the target of improper imitations. For many foreign investors, this is a sign of a helpful new attitude in India. In the end, in-house counsel should carefully review what intellectual property assets their companies own or license and evaluate whether India's intellectual property laws may pose a serious barrier to any potential investment plans.

POINT THREE

REGIONALISM WITHIN THE WORLD'S LARGEST DEMOCRACY

Like China, India is not really one country. It is made up of diverse economic regions, each with different strengths and weaknesses.

Aside from economics, strong regional political sentiments exist throughout India, and they can influence how local government officials view individual foreign investment projects. The current winners, representing the regions most open to foreign investment, are Central and Southern India. This is where thousands of outsourced service centers and technology ventures exist, many of which are examples of targeted foreign direct investments. Cities like Bangalore, Chennai, Mysore, and Hyderabad have attracted not just call centers but also IT research and development projects that are backed by multinational corporations. India's Silicon Valley is booming and open for business.

On the Western coast, Mumbai (formerly Bombay) is both the major commercial port and the financial center of India. Most of the multifaceted commerce that goes on between India and the Middle East wends its way through Mumbai's port and banks. In Central and Northern India, Delhi is the federal and governmental heart of the country and is always trying to attract additional technology companies. There are five other major regions of India, each of which has its own particular strengths and weaknesses. Consequently, a company must be geographically and economically savvy when analyzing where best to locate an investment in India. One suggestion is to research in advance those locations where other foreign companies in similar industries have already put down roots and had success.

Point Four

Due Diligence Issues When Evaluating Indian Service Providers or Joint Venture Partners

Any in-house lawyer asked to prepare a joint venture agreement or a service provider agreement between an Indian party and a Western company should begin by asking fifteen key questions. The answers to these questions will help in the evaluation of prospective service suppliers or joint venture partners in India.

1. How long has the Indian company been in business? What is its general reputation? If it is a recent start-up venture, who stands behind it, and are the owners reliable? Remember, many Indian companies are privately held, and financial and historical information may be hard to independently verify.
2. How well capitalized is the Indian company you are considering as a potential partner or target?
3. Is the Indian company a stand-alone company, or is it part of a related group of companies? Are there any related companies that are financially strong, and will they be available to offer support financially and otherwise? What about cross-guarantees of performance in the event your potential partner is capitally deficient?
4. Does the Indian company and its management have any prior practical experience with foreign investors, such as a prior joint venture or contractual relationship? Were those engagements successful? Consider talking to references of those foreign investors as part of the due diligence process.
5. Were any key employees of the Indian company educated in the United States or Europe, or did they live for a period of time in the West (aside from a university setting)? Do they understand American and European business practices and expectations?
6. Has the Indian company worked with other companies (Indian or otherwise) in the past that might be considered potential competitors?
7. Does the Indian company have any prior experience providing services to the particular market sector or customers you wish to serve?
8. What is the size of the Indian labor force currently employed in the company? What skill set do those employees possess? Does the company have a good reputation for treating its workers well?
9. Is English fluency among the Indian workers important to your company's needs? Is English widely used by those in the geographic region in India where you hope to locate your operations?

10. What level of wages does the Indian company pay its workers? What is the average tenure of an employee at the Indian company?
11. In the geographic region where you might expect to set up your Indian operations, are there adequate pools of potential workers who possess the requisite skills you will need? Can you project an adequate pool in the middle and long terms?
12. Is the location of the Indian company in a part of India where ethnic or religious tensions are likely to arise? Is there a history of work stoppages in this area?
13. How do employees at the Indian company get to work? Is adequate public transportation available, or must the Indian employer supply specialized transportation or other arrangements for its workers? Is local traffic manageable? This is not a trivial point if workers depend on public transportation. Is housing an issue?
14. How does the Indian company maintain its business records, and does its financial and accounting data conform to the needs of your U.S. operations?
15. If you expect to conduct operations in India on a 24-7 basis, can the Indian company guarantee its level of performance to this standard? What background experience in operating 24-7 does the company have?

Point Five

Key Contractual Issues When Outsourcing to an Indian Entity

At the most basic level, Western-trained lawyers will find themselves comfortable with the legal system as it exists in India. The reason is today's India has its roots with the English, who colonized and controlled India for generations until it became an independent country after World War II. The English approach to the common law and court systems, and a regulatory approach toward business, left an indelible imprint on India long after the English left the country in 1947.

Once you have identified and vetted the best qualified partner or outsourcing candidate in India, the next step is drafting a detailed contract to outline the obligations between your company and the Indian enterprise. You should begin by following the same steps you would if you were drafting in an American or European context. It is essential to carefully negotiate and outline the relationship with your potential Indian partner or supplier because the Indians will expect to receive a detailed legal document outlining the rights and obligations of the parties. The following key points should be evaluated when drafting a contract to outsource service needs to an Indian enterprise.

A. *Defining Services.* Indians will closely rely on and adhere to the language of a contract. This is why definitions in a contract with an Indian company are important and should be as complete and unambiguous as possible. For example, clearly define the type of "services" that you would expect the Indian company to provide to the foreign partner. Do not exclude anything from the definition. At least, the definition should include minimum daily/weekly/monthly service levels acceptable to the U.S. company. Quantify wherever possible all criteria that will be used for evaluation of the Indian entity.
B. *Best Efforts.* The requirements of using one's "best efforts" is a potential concern when the two parties to the contract are geographically distant. For this reason, define *best efforts* in a quantitative sense wherever possible when mandating what is expected of the Indian company and its employees. Include what levels of quality performance are minimally required and proscribe what steps will be taken over time by the Indian company to correct any errors or subpar performance issues.
C. *Invoice Disputes.* Again because of the distance between the parties, put in the contract the procedures to follow when handling invoices. If appropriate, determine in advance if there are any types of invoices that need to be treated differently. Set forth in your agreement the specific time frame in which any invoice disputes must be brought to the attention of the other party and the method by which disputes will be resolved.

D. *Guarantees of Performance.* An American- or European-based company should consider demanding guarantees of contractual obligations by an Indian company. If its ability to perform in the future is questionable or if it lacks adequate financial resources to resolve problems, a guarantee makes sense. Consider requiring a letter of credit or standby letter of credit from the Indian entity to assure its performance. Having a documented guarantee in place will enable you to put pressure on the Indian company if and when problems arise or disruptions in service occur. Make sure the letter of credit issued on behalf of the Indian party remains in effect until after the underlying contract terminates, so the termination of the contract may not be asserted by the one party as a basis to void any corporate obligations secured by the letter of credit.

E. *Onsite and Offsite Supervision.* As most successful multinationals have learned in India, China, and elsewhere, continuous oversight of foreign operations is vital. In the contract, provide that the U.S. company has the right at its own expense to conduct permanent or episodic inspections of the facility in India. This can include the right to oversee and approve the hiring, retention, and evaluation of service personnel. The U.S. company should insist on full and unrestricted access (online remote) for all computers, telephones, storage devices, and related sites on a 24-7 basis that affect business activities.

F. *Confidentiality.* Because Indian laws and courts do not provide the same levels of protection for proprietary business information as exists in the United States, a carefully drawn contract dealing with confidentiality is essential. Both parties must contractually agree that all proprietary information of the venture will remain confidential during the term of the contract and for a defined period after termination. As recommended earlier, carefully define what you consider "proprietary information" and "trade secrets." Require the return of all files and related materials (and copies thereof) in a timely manner upon termination of the Indian supplier for whatever cause.

G. *Force Majeure.* Do not try to use a "form" force majeure clause. In my experience, there is no force majeure clause that works in all circumstances, particularly in India. The U.S. company must specifically insist on the right to terminate the agreement if a force majeure event occurs and make sure the clause reflects the terms of the underlying contract. For example, the parties must determine how long such an event can continue (i.e., 15, 30, or 45 days) before termination is effective and whether such events can be cumulative. In the case of India, you may find the time to cure needs to be longer than normal elsewhere because obtaining the approval of an Indian bureaucrat can take unreasonable lengths of time, depending on the needs of the parties.

H. *Termination of the Indian Supplier by the U.S. Company.* As with parts of the contract, carefully list each of the events which may trigger termination of the Indian company. Must the U.S. company require "cause" for termination? It is wise to keep the provisions for termination in mind when drafting the definitions of *services* and *best efforts* in the contract.

I. *Deconversion.* Deconversion is an essential issue to address in any contract, because sometimes a company selects the wrong supplier or partner. A well-drafted contract will provide for the possibility that the U.S. company may at some future time elect to switch its business to an alternative service supplier. In this case, you need to contractually require the Indian company to continue supplying services to your company until such a transfer (conversion) is complete. Consider tying this obligation to the letter of credit to be supplied by the Indian company.

J. *Indemnification.* In the event the indemnification of the Indian company is not satisfactory, ask for the indemnification of a related company. See other sections of this chapter for further guidance.

K. *Limitations of Liability.* Negotiate whether you will accept limitations of liability on the Indian company. Even if the liability is limited, you still need a viable entity capable of paying damages in the event of default. One approach is to see whether any insurance coverage is available to cover possible claims and related costs. If insurance is reasonably priced, consider purchasing the insurance as opposed to relying on dispute resolution in Indian courts or through arbitration.

L. *Dispute Resolution.* My advice is to avoid using Indian courts for resolving commercial disputes if at all possible. Binding third-party arbitration is almost always preferable. If the other party is flexible, negotiate the requirement that any arbitration be conducted outside of India. If the Indians refuse to arbitrate in the United States or Western Europe, suggest using Asian-based alternative arbitration tribunals. I can recommend two good alternatives: the Hong Kong International Arbitration Centre (HKIAC) and the Singapore International Arbitration Centre (SIAC). Both are well respected and have long histories of impartial dispute resolution. You will find either the SIAC or the HKIAC to be more acceptable to the Indian supplier than a venue in the West. As always, state in your contract that arbitrations are to be conducted in the English language.

M. *Change in Control.* It is also wise to consider a contractual provision that states that if a "change in control" of the Indian company (as defined in the agreement) occurs, then such change of control provides a legitimate basis for the U.S. company to terminate the contract if it so elects. A contract should also specifically prohibit any assignment of the obligations of the Indian company to a third party without prior written consent of the U.S. entity. Assignment is an area of particular risk in India because the assignee may not have the same resources or quality as the original party to the contract.

N. *Termination by Election of the Indian Company.* In the event the Indian company is entitled to and desires to terminate the relationship, require adequate advance notice so an orderly transition is possible without disruption of service. Again, try to tie the ongoing performance of the Indian company to the letter of credit or standby letter of credit. You may want to provide for a short-term (sixty days or less) standby so the managers of each party may meet to see if any dispute can be resolved.

Point Six
Tips on Negotiating in India

India is a far more diverse and challenging place to negotiate than other parts of Asia, including China. While the Hindustan and English languages are widely spoken in India, there are still more than 1,250 individual dialects and languages used daily throughout the country. In addition to the complexities different languages can pose, in-house counsel must be aware of the heightened sensitivities that exist among ethnic and subculture groups in India. If these issues are not properly recognized and addressed during the negotiation process, problems may occur in the future. Consequently, I strongly recommend that foreign investors in India retain local experts who can advise them throughout the negotiation process.

When preparing for a negotiation in India, recognize that at the most fundamental level the Indian people are extremely proud and sensitive. Ironically, the smaller the job or transaction, the more it is likely to be a problem. Minor public officials in India will hold up the process with great frequency. This goes back to pride and their desire to be recognized as important. While a perceived slight in China may evoke an unexpected reaction, the same misstep in India can cause an even more extreme reaction. As a general rule, I have found the Indians are more emotional than the Chinese and more likely to both take offense to a perceived wrong and to keep their frustration a secret. There are few second chances in India, which is why it is so vitally important to prepare in advance for negotiations with an Indian party and to set forth in a clear and unambiguous manner the key issues to be addressed. Say everything three times and then ask them to repeat it back to you to confirm understanding and acceptance. The bottom line? Avoid jokes, religious references, comments about politics or corruption, and personal inquiries both inside and outside of the conference room. The one exception I have found is that inquiring about someone's family is a very nice gesture.

Indians are not stoic like the Chinese or Japanese. It is a mistake, however, to misinterpret the intensity of the Indian psyche for weakness. While Indians are a highly rational people, their emotional reactions to perceived slights are immediate and direct. In India, a problem that seems minor at first blush can quickly escalate into a major crisis. Therefore, I always recommend during business dealings in India that information be presented in the form of written data and hard facts and that emotion rarely, if ever, be injected into the discussions. Unless you have known your Indian counterparts for a long time and have developed a truly personal relationship, always accentuate formality over familiarity.

Furthermore, because of India's diverse religious culture, Westerners must be careful to ensure that nothing they say can be viewed as a perceived slight related to any religious group. Because of their country's diverse culture and size, the Indians over a long time have evolved a culture among themselves that manages to maintain tight control over ethnic and religious strife by practicing this type of sensitivity.

Point Seven
Litigation and Arbitration in India

The government in India is a federation made up of six union territories and twenty-nine separate states. Within its federated system, India has a single integrated court system, which is designed to administer the laws of the states and union territories.

The major criticism of India's court system is that it is very slow to render final and binding decisions in commercial cases. There are multiple factors contributing to this; some are political, some are historical, and some are uniquely cultural, such as an attitude among some Indian lawyers that delaying a case for the sole purpose of delay is not necessarily inappropriate. Whatever the reasons, the fact is that India's court system is rarely voluntarily selected by Indian companies or foreign investors if they want to resolve a commercial dispute in a timely manner. As explained elsewhere in this chapter, commercial disputes in India are resolved not by the court system but rather by submission to binding arbitration. Unless there is a significant reason to choose otherwise, when drafting commercial contracts in India or with Indian parties, you should demand that the parties adopt arbitration as the way to resolve commercial disputes.

Point Eight
The Indian Style of Management

The successful management of operations in India requires a unique mind-set, whether the management is part of a joint venture or a foreign investment. My suggestion is that managing in the "Indian style" is the best approach. By this I mean that management decisions within Indian companies are traditionally hierarchical and done in a formal manner. Decisions are typically made within the management structure and rarely imposed from the outside. The upshot of how Indians react to managers is that you will need to devote significant time and effort to building a "team" within a business that reflects Indian sensitivities and character. Attempting to bring outsiders (non-Indians) into the decision-making process will be met with strong opposition by the Indians, who will resist and find it offensive (unless they are at the top, and then they will welcome the attention).

In dealing with Indian employees and managers on a one-on-one basis, you will find they are almost always anxious to share their ideas. When asked to participate within a business structure, Indians will enthusiastically put forward their suggestions. You will not have to work to draw them out. In fact, you will insult them if you do not ask. By recognizing this national desire and willingness to participate, owners of an entity in India will be much more successful if they convey to the Indian workers and lower-level executives that they are respected. Praise is *always* a good idea!

The concept of *face*, or saving face, which is often discussed in Asia, takes on a particularly high level of importance in India. When trying to conceive and structure a major project in the United States, it is common to put together a small team and ask it to brainstorm ideas, and then come back and discuss them with higher-level management. This lack of specification (a wide-open assignment) is often embraced as a challenge in the American context. In India, I have found the opposite to be true. The lack of specifications as to what a team is expected to accomplish and when they are expected to produce results is not well accepted. In my experience, when dealing with an Indian team, the more details you provide about the type of project and how and when it is to be accomplished and why it should be done a specific way, the better chance there is of having it done correctly and in a timely manner. While Indian workers are as smart, accomplished, hardworking, and insightful as any workers around the world, they are not always as focused when interpreting and filling in the gaps as might be the case in Western countries. If you leave the decisions to the Indian team, they will tend to overpromise and underperform because culturally they do not want to disappoint their superiors. Being thoroughly direct and detailed from the start will produce better results in the end from your Indian workers.

In short, managing in India, if done by adopting the Indian style, will provide the best chance for success. In India, as in China, it is better to identify and hire top Indian executives to manage and run your operations as opposed to bringing in expatriates from the United States or elsewhere and hoping they will succeed. Who better to manage Indians than Indians?

Point Nine

Law Firms in India and Working with Indian Lawyers

The Indian government and Indian bar groups have strongly resisted allowing multinational law firms to set up full-service offices or form joint ventures in India. Today India finds itself under major international pressure to change its current stance on admitting foreign lawyers into the country, and there is some indication that Indian attitudes are indeed changing for the better. Nevertheless, at the time this chapter is being written, there are no major alternatives for foreign companies looking to retain legal talent in India except to hire established Indian law firms. The top Indian law firms are made up of superbly trained lawyers, many of whom were educated in the United Kingdom and elsewhere. I strongly recommend that you personally travel to India and interview prospective law firms that may work with your company. Many of the larger Indian law firms maintain offices in multiple cities throughout India. During your interviews, evaluate what level of experience their lawyers have in dealing with non-Indian companies and their level of IT expertise. Since many Indian lawyers have received their legal training outside India, you will find they are quite sensitive to the needs of American and European companies.

Conclusion

While India shows great promise for the future, it must confront six major challenges successfully if it hopes to reach its full potential.

Challenge One

Even today, India's population remains predominantly agricultural. Those who live and work in India's agricultural areas are among the poorest in the country. One reason is that the Indian agricultural system is antiquated and does not take advantage of advances in agribusiness. The problems go beyond mere inefficiencies. India has to develop a more comprehensive approach to efficient agricultural production and land ownership if it hopes to meet its needs in the future.

Challenge Two

Above all else, the one thing China has done well over the last thirty years is to build significant infrastructure throughout the country. You will see new and highly efficient roads, ports, bridges, railroads, and high-speed trains throughout China, especially in the coastal areas. This tremendous investment has allowed China to become a world leader in manufacturing. India is exactly the opposite. All of India's ports are antiquated, and its road system is poor. The lack of bridges, highways, and adequate rail lines continues to inhibit India's desire to rapidly expand its economy. What India must do over the next twenty years is devote very high levels of capital to funding infrastructure projects. This is particularly important for leading Indian companies because world-class competitors within their sectors may find the ability to move their products outside India due to infrastructure weaknesses is a real challenge.

Challenge Three

India's system of higher education is turning out world-class graduates in a variety of sectors. The problem remains, however, that the demand in India for educated managers and businesspeople continues to outpace the number of successful graduates produced by Indian universities.

Challenge Four

India remains the largest democracy in the world with an extremely vibrant and diverse group of nationalities and interests. In many ways, India's strength can also be a weakness. The democratic process tends to slow down fundamental decision making because there are vested interests that may oppose changing the current system.

Challenge Five

Religious and ethnic strife is not new to India or to other countries in the region, but the challenge in India is not just internal strife between the Muslims and the Hindus. The situation is exacerbated by a large Muslim population to the north in Pakistan and Afghanistan. The strife along the border areas has continued for years, and the more unstable Pakistan becomes from a political and military standpoint, the more strongly the Indians will become concerned about their neighbors. This kind of uncertainty leads to problems for foreign companies looking for a safe place to invest.

Challenge Six

Without question, India's largest challenge is its rapidly growing population. While China has controlled its population well over the last forty years (albeit by questionable methods), India has moved in the opposite direction. In short, India's rate of population growth is out of control. Somehow the Indian government has to slow down the population growth, or else annual economic growth of 5% or 6% will be more than canceled out by the population demands.

CHAPTER FIVE

CHINA—THE EMERGING COLOSSUS

China has blossomed into the world's largest hub for automobile manufacturing and assembly because of exploding demand by Chinese consumers. An American auto parts supplier, hoping to cash in on this trend, visited China to explore the possibility of a joint venture with a Chinese parts manufacturer. Negotiations between the American supplier and the Chinese manufacturer stumbled along for three months. Seven negotiators sat on the Chinese side of the bargaining table along with two or three others filling chairs in the back of the room. Finally, all of the major points necessary for the joint venture agreement were resolved, except for one: Who would have majority control over the joint venture once it went into operation? Without majority control, the board of directors of the American company would veto the deal.

On the final day, the lead American negotiator declared that majority control over the joint venture was a deal breaker. Unless there was a concession, the Americans were going home—it was the point of no return. This demand was presented directly to the main Chinese negotiator, who held a very senior title and position within the Chinese enterprise. Upon hearing the Americans' demand, the Chinese called an immediate halt to the negotiations. At first the Chinese team conferred with each other, then suddenly turned their backs to the American team and walked to the rear of the room. Sitting in the corner was an old man wearing an ill-fitting Mao suit. He had been sitting there by himself for days saying nothing, just observing the negotiations. Everyone on the American side had assumed the old man was some low-level clerk or hanger-on. The Americans were wrong. As it turned out, the unassuming man in the rumpled Mao suit was a very highly ranking Chinese official who held the ultimate power to decide whether the deal would go forward. After months of dinners, meetings, and endless negotiations, the Americans were shocked to discover that the top dog was actually sitting silently in the back of the room.

Economists always speak about the need for "transparency" in business. They look for signs or events that can make it clearer to outsiders what is happening in the murky world of international business. But, as the old man in the Mao suit proved, transparency in Asia—and particularly in China—is elusive.

If you are an in-house counsel providing advice to a company hoping to do business in China, you face a series of daunting challenges. Whether you are a novice to China or have visited dozens of times, China never fails to surprise. No one is really an expert on China. A friend of mine once put it well: "If you visit China once, you think you have learned enough to write a book. If you visit China three times, you can write a chapter. If you have been to China as many times as I have, you have trouble composing a single sentence." Basically, the reality is that China is so vast, diverse, and complex that no one—not even the Chinese themselves—can truly understand it all.

While you may think the circumstances of your company's efforts to conduct business with the Chinese are unique, I have discovered over the years that ten fundamental issues touch upon almost every transaction in one way or another. This chapter describes those ten issues that you as in-house counsel need to understand before consummating a deal with the Chinese.

ISSUE ONE

THE ROLE OF THE CHINESE GOVERNMENT IN BUSINESS TRANSACTIONS

As the true story about the old man in the Mao suit highlights, transparency in China is a never-ending challenge. During any negotiation with the Chinese, whether it is conducted within China or elsewhere, you must constantly assess the individuals with whom you are dealing and try to figure out whether they really have the power to make key decisions. What you often discover is that the power to make the important business decisions is held elsewhere, not with the negotiators you have come to know so intimately.

The reason the old man was so influential in that negotiation is the fact that his influence went far beyond the corporate position he held in the Chinese enterprise. What American and European negotiators frequently miss is that individuals who hold high corporate positions within Chinese enterprises are also often closely aligned with the Chinese Communist Party (or some sector of the Chinese government). Accept the fact that when negotiating in China, there is often an invisible and indispensable player at the table; that is, the role played by the Chinese government in determining the ultimate outcome. Sometimes the involvement of the Party in a Chinese enterprise is openly disclosed; sometimes it is opaque. My visits to China over twenty-five years have taught me that negotiating in China is a bit like shadowboxing while never quite knowing where the shadow is.

This phenomenon is not unique to China. It is a mistake to assume that other governments around the world don't likewise aid private enterprises within their national borders. French government officials are famous for exercising their authority to stave off bids by multinationals seeking an unfriendly takeover of or merger with prominent French companies. Another example is Thailand.

Thailand is a country with a constitutional monarchy, and while the role of the king from an outside perspective appears largely ceremonial, King Bhumibol Adulyadej and the Royal Family are extremely powerful politically. Several times over the last thirty years when crises have arisen within the Thai elected government, it was only through the intervention of the king that those conflicts were resolved without escalating into serious dislocations. For more than four decades, the Ministry of International Trade & Industry (MITI) in Japan, now renamed and known as METI, exerted massive influence in determining what foreign investments were funded and given priority by the Japanese bureaucracy. The same has been true in Korea ever since the end of the Korean conflict. The powerful Korean conglomerates known as *chaebols* have benefited from the political influence exerted behind the scenes by Korean government bureaucrats. In the international sphere, most governments simply cannot and rarely do not resist the urge to help their local companies over foreign multinational corporations seeking to compete with them.

You have to appreciate that it was less than three decades ago when everything in China was a government-owned enterprise. The move toward privatization in China is still relatively young, which means that government officials at the local, provincial, and national levels in China can and do exert influence over what would otherwise appear to be private business transactions. Why do you need to understand this? The reason is, when a large number of Chinese government enterprises became privatized over the last twenty years, the local and provincial (state) governments in China retained some level of ownership interest in those companies. Even though a Chinese enterprise may appear to be totally privatized, remaining ownership interests by Chinese government entities are not always obvious.

I recommend that, early in the negotiation stages with a Chinese party, you not only investigate its current financial strengths and ability to provide services but also take a look into its background and ownership. Ask key questions. Where did it originally begin? Was it at one time wholly owned by a local or provincial government? Is there any equity that the government may have retained within the enterprise? These are the kinds of questions that should be explored early on to avoid later misunderstandings and potential issues that might ultimately keep the deal from moving forward.

Another example of government involvement in China can arise in the area of ownership and financing of a Chinese venture. Even when a Chinese enterprise may appear to have no government ownership, take a look at the banks or other financial institutions that have over time lent money to the Chinese enterprise. Many Chinese banks, particularly local and regional, are heavily controlled or influenced by Chinese government officials. These officials have the power to "suggest" to whom a local or regional bank can make a loan and even strongly influence on a more macro level how and when banks in China can lend at all. On January 21, 2010, China's central government halted most lending by Chinese banks on one day's notice after the announcement of more than 10% growth in the fourth quarter of 2009. Because the Chinese wanted to control the possibility of future inflation, it directed banks to stop lending. This shows how powerful the government is in directing the Chinese economy. Because of this, you as counsel should always carefully examine the web of financial relationships existing between the Chinese enterprise and its sources of financing within China. One way to accomplish this is to retain an independent third party to privately find out about your potential Chinese partner or supplier before beginning negotiations. You can be sure that when one Chinese company is considering doing a venture with another, they will conduct the same kind of background investigation.

In short, always assume there is either a direct or indirect involvement by local Chinese officials in your target enterprise in China. The more you discover up front, the less likely you are to encounter problems in the final stages of a negotiation.

Issue Two

The Specter of Corruption

In my opinion, China has been tagged with an undeserved reputation as a nation with significant institutional corruption. The reality is that every nation in the world, including the United States, suffers from some degree of corruption at the local, state, and federal levels.

While China has a history of corruption, the landscape is changing because of China's leader Hu Jintao. Since he has been in power, the government has rigorously targeted institutional corruption within China. For example, in 2010 a former Chinese judge was sentenced to life imprisonment and all of his property confiscated for having taken bribes while deputy head of the Supreme People's Court. This prosecution is not an isolated incident. The *Financial Times* on July 8, 2010, had a large color photograph above the fold of Wen Qiang. Wen had been the director of the Chonqing Judicial Bureau and before that deputy head of the Police Bureau. He was convicted of taking bribes, hiding financial assets, and shielding organized crime from prosecution. He was executed, and the Chinese publicly acknowledged this in the most public manner. The point is that, under Hu, the Chinese government is now taking serious steps to root out corruption at all levels. The reason is simple—corruption that influences the awarding of contracts, licenses, or preferential treatment is detrimental to the Chinese economy. Corruption encourages the awarding of projects to companies that are not necessarily the best or even the least expensive. Corruption is bad for any government, particularly in a rapidly emerging economy like China. The Chinese leadership recognizes this and is determined to combat it across the board.

While in-house counsel reading this book already knows about the Foreign Corrupt Practices Act (FCPA) and how it prohibits U.S. companies and individuals from illegally conducting business overseas, it is equally important to recognize that local laws in China (as in many other countries) also prohibit bribery or improper payments to government officials. These laws must be taken seriously. To highlight the extent of its commitment, a number of high-level officials have been put to death by the central government in China for significant corruption. This would rarely, if ever, have happened in the past—things are definitely changing.

All this is not to suggest that corruption does not exist in China. It does. However, foreign companies, European and American alike, must strongly resist all requests for illegal payments when they go to China.

From doing business in China over the years, I know that foreign investors *do not* have to make illegal payments or authorize improper actions in order to successfully conduct business in China. The trick is to avoid any and all illegal activities from the beginning. Obviously for American companies, their subsidiaries, and related entities around the world, any such payments to Chinese government officials or members of the Chinese Communist Party are a violation of the FCPA. The reality is that European and American companies that have engaged in improper payments end up in a trap in which they are forced to make these kinds of payments forever. Without question, this is a very delicate issue that requires close examination by counsel when advising executives on conducting business in China. The bottom line is that such payments are a violation of the FCPA, a direct violation of Chinese anticorruption statutes, and counter to the desire of the Chinese government to eliminate, or at least significantly control, corruption at the local, provincial, and federal levels.

Issue Three

China's Vast Economic and Geographic Diversity

It is a mistake to think about China as a single country. There are at least half a dozen distinct regions in China that boast different dialects, diverse economies, and unique local political structures.

Foreign investors often fail to appreciate how different it is conducting business in one geographic area of China versus another. The process of selecting which is the best region to do business in China is complex. Take note—the offer of a tax holiday or other incentive by a local government should not in itself be enough to convince a foreign company to invest or do a project in that specific location. While taxes are a factor, it is more important to, for example, find out whether appropriate infrastructure exists, including power and ports, transportation links, and basic resources, in the location where you are considering your foreign investment.

While China has approximately 1.3 billion people, about 450 million are living within a hundred miles or so of the coastline, stretching from Hong Kong and Macao in the south up through Beijing and Tianjin to Harbin in the far north. The rest of China, which comprises the central, northern, and western areas, has about 900 million people. Unlike the Chinese living in the more prosperous coastal areas, much of China is very agricultural and thus quite poor in comparison. A strong tension exists between the wealthy coastal Chinese and the poorer Chinese in the internal provinces.

Issue Four

The Joint Venture versus the Wholly Owned Subsidiary in China

For American and European companies that decide to engage in business in China, the two most common scenarios are (1) setting up a joint venture with a Chinese company or (2) establishing a formal wholly owned operation in China. A subsidiary in China is most often referred to as a wholly owned foreign enterprise (WOFE). To understand the options available in China today, it helps to look back at how foreign direct investment in China evolved.

In 1972, former President Richard M. Nixon's unexpected and historic visit to China surprised everyone because it opened up for the first time in half a century the possibility of commercial activities between American companies and the Chinese. However, few substantive business relationships between China and the West developed over the next six years. One reason was that under Chinese laws and regulations at the time, direct foreign investment into China was virtually impossible. Up until then, the role China played in the international marketplace (excluding Hong Kong and Macao) was extremely limited. Less than 10% of national income before 1980 was involved with foreign trade.

This all changed in 1978 when China publicly announced an "open door" policy that was aimed at attracting much-needed foreign capital and technologies, particularly from investors in the United States and Europe. China was poor and felt the only way to reverse this was to invite outsiders who would bring money, technology, and expertise. This radical policy was a direct result of actions initiated by Deng Xiaoping, who forced China's leadership to reverse its traditional opposition to foreign trade and investment. Deng believed foreign investment and technology were the only way that a modern, industrial country could evolve over a short period of time. Over the next quarter century, China has periodically introduced new laws and implemented complex sets of incentives specifically designed to govern and encourage foreign investment activities. From 1979 to 1986, a total of 7,500 foreign investment contracts and memorandums of understanding (MOUs) were signed in China with a value of approximately $19.1 billion USD. Since 1986, the number of investments has increased thirtyfold.

The death of Deng Xiaoping on February 19, 1997, marked the final transition to a new and younger generation of leadership in China. Deng's handpicked successor, Jiang Zemin, promised to uphold the economic revolution initiated by Deng. This held true through 2002, when the Chinese leadership again changed. After a two-year transition, in September 2004 Jiang Zemin formally ceded all of his official positions to his successor Hu Jintao. Over the last half decade, Hu has continued the official government policy of his predecessors which encourages foreign investment in China. This continual policy is why China has experienced such dramatic growth since the 1980s.

Beginning in the 1970s until the early 1990s, most investments in China required some type of joint venture. During this time, Chinese laws strongly encouraged the joint venture vehicle. Beginning in the early 1990s, the Chinese government felt a pushback by foreign investors, many of whom felt they no longer needed or desired to have Chinese partners and wanted to do business in China on their own terms. To avoid discouraging foreign companies, the Chinese government revised its laws on investments and allowed foreign companies under certain circumstances to form their own wholly owned foreign enterprises (WOFEs) in China. If you travel in China today, you will observe increasing numbers of foreign companies that have been in China for a long time moving away from their existing joint ventures and toward adopting the WOFE format. While obviously there are advantages and disadvantages to both structures, the WOFE appears to be where most foreign investors are headed.

That said, however, there are certain industries in China where foreign investors are prohibited from wholly owned operations. In such sectors, even when establishing a WOFE, you may find the Chinese government has a strong influence and you are pushed to accept a strong Chinese partner.

Because China has been a member of the World Trade Organization (WTO) for some time now, the trend toward foreign investors preferring wholly owned subsidiaries has taken on a life of its own. WTO officials have urged the Chinese government to rescind its old system of granting a virtual monopoly to domestic Chinese companies dealing with importing, exporting, and distribution. It is now possible for foreign investors and non-Chinese multinational corporations to ship goods to China's mainland without the requirement of going through a Chinese-owned and controlled trading company. This is a significant change for the Chinese. One example of a foreign company that has embraced doing business in China is Walmart.

Another development to think about is the minimum capital required under Chinese law to set up commercial enterprises, which includes sales and retail outlets, wholesalers, and franchises. The minimum levels were reduced significantly in recent years. Yet another example is franchising in China, which was once prohibited but is now more open to foreign investors. These and other reforms will make China more available and attractive to smaller foreign investors, who in the past found it difficult to explore Chinese opportunities for many reasons.

ISSUE FIVE

OUTSOURCING YOUR MANUFACTURING REQUIREMENTS TO CHINA

Chinese labor is no longer the least expensive in the world. This means that China's drive over the last twenty years to develop a very strong infrastructure, including ports, railways, and highways, has become quite important in that it benefits companies looking to manufacture products in China for sale both within the country and into export markets. There are eight factors that you as in-house counsel should consider when reviewing the prospects for outsourcing manufacturing to China.

Factor One: Government Involvement in Your Business

Determine where in China you expect to do business, and carefully investigate what government bodies will influence or regulate your activities before you make a decision where to locate. Important questions to ask are as follows.

Will the central government or a specific ministry have direct regulatory influence over your anticipated activities in China?

1. Do you expect the Chinese government or a ministry to be a potential buyer of your products or services? How will this affect your marketing activities? (*Note*: If the Chinese will buy your products, they can accelerate the approval requirements.)
2. Is mandatory licensing or prior government clearance required in order to sell in China? (*Example*: Pharmaceuticals or medical equipment must be preapproved before sales in China are authorized.) (*Note*: Licensing can be a complex and lengthy process.)
3. Should you initiate contacts with key government officials to explore issues prior to formal negotiations? (*Note*: This is always a good idea because of the role government officials may play in the approval process for your investment.)
4. Is it advisable to utilize a Chinese intermediary to interface with government officials before, during, and after negotiations? Does the intermediary have a preexisting relationship with those officials?

Will the provincial government(s) in China exercise influence over how your business is conducted in their jurisdiction?

1. Registration requirements?
2. Licensure? (*Note*: You may have to deal with provincial as well as local officials)

What regulations will influence your activities in China?

Some examples of regulations you will deal with are local labor laws, environmental requirements, and taxation statutes.

Factor Two: Tax Considerations

1. For any intended business activities in China (national, provincial, local), analyze what tax statutes are involved and what filings may be required.
2. Joint ventures can present a variety of potential tax pitfalls for foreign investors. For example, some Chinese joint ventures

with non-Chinese investors are initially approved with preferential tax treatment (tax holdings) offered as an incentive for investment in a particular geographic region. Research in advance what the dissolution of a joint venture or buyout of a local partner at a later point might have on your tax status, such as the future recapture of previously deferred taxes.

3. Determine whether as a foreign investor in China you are permitted to operate without a local partner. If your Chinese joint venture is failing, line up a new partner before initiating discussions to terminate your existing partner. Otherwise, your tax treatment may be drastically altered.
4. In most Asian countries, you are prohibited from transferring assets from one entity to another until all formal notifications are filed and mandated government approvals are issued.
5. Foreign investors entering China are now taxed on the same basis (with some exceptions) as Chinese companies. This leveled playing field is a relatively recent development and makes the "Let's Make a Deal" approach by local governments trying to attract investors far less important.

Factor Three: Accounting Issues

Whether you elect to invest in a joint venture or set up a WOFE in China, various accounting issues will influence the transaction. Consider the following questions.

Will the accounting methods used in China be consistent with your American or European-based accounting systems?

Note: This is an area where you will be challenged at first.

Will problems arise with U.S.-based tax returns in the event of a dissolution or assumption of a local party's joint venture interest?

Note: This can be tricky and extremely costly in the event of an unhappy breakup. You should perform in-depth periodic audits to ensure that you truly know about the success of or problems with your joint venture.

Factor Four: Employee and Labor Issues

Employee and labor issues in a Chinese joint venture are time consuming and less predictable than in a U.S.-based joint venture. Here are some unique issues to consider:

1. American companies commonly assign one or more of their executives to work overseas in a foreign joint venture. These expatriate employees are authorized to work in a foreign country based solely on their direct and active involvement at the managerial level in the joint venture. To the extent the legal status of a joint venture changes, you may discover that the immigration status of your expatriate managers is adversely affected. Often the "right of abode" and ability to work is granted for a set period and subject to periodic review by foreign labor and/or immigration officials. This possibility mandates advance examination and ongoing monitoring in order to avoid unpleasant surprises.
2. Foreign labor statutes impose obligations on joint venture employers. Be aware that terminating a joint venture or transferring its assets to another entity (or a new entity) may create separate sets of problems.
   a. *Executives*: In restructuring a joint venture or buying out a partner, an executive or director may be entitled to termination benefits based upon local labor laws which can take precedence over contractual obligations with the venture itself. For example, where foreign corporate regulations require that a local person serve on a board of directors, such a director may be entitled to compensation (even if it is a part-time or titular position) in the event a joint venture is restructured or terminated.
   b. *Professional Staff*: Professional employees in China have statutory rights. Reviewing the alternatives with local legal counsel is encouraged early in the process because professional staff in a foreign joint venture understand their rights under local statutes and will act accordingly.

c. *Workers*: Whether workers are represented in their activities by labor unions varies from country to country based upon local laws. Labor unions do exist in China and may assume a role in determining wages, working conditions, and terminations. In Asian countries where labor unions are not a factor, the statutory rights of laborers are usually triggered in the event of dissolution of a joint venture or change of control.

Factor Five: Licensed Technology

When doing business overseas, U.S.-based companies commonly license their technologies to joint ventures in which they have an equity stake. License agreements can facilitate the legitimate transfer of royalties (hard currency) out of a country back to the United States. Research in advance the implications of technology licensing into China. For example, will U.S. governmental oversight or approvals be required under U.S. export control laws and regulations?

Factor Six: Banking and Financial Concerns

Despite recent public announcements to the contrary, China still has a currency in the renminbi (yuan), which is largely inconvertible and does not "float." This means the government is involved if you want to take profits or money out of China that were earned in the local currency. This poses challenges for foreign companies doing business in China whether they are part of a joint venture or a WOFE.

1. Consider bank loans. Will the dissolution of a joint venture or the sale of interest to the U.S. partner by the Chinese accelerate any loan payment obligations or create related problems under existing loan covenants?
2. Letters of credit are the most common form of transferring money and paying obligations in international business trans-

actions. It is critical that nothing adversely affects the ongoing viability or enforceability of letters of credit (either incoming or outgoing). This will arise in an inamicable breakup of a joint venture because one party has an economic or personal interest in not supporting the viability of the surviving entity.
3. Parent companies in international transactions are frequently asked to guarantee performance obligations of their ventures through various financial mechanisms. This is particularly true for those involved in international construction and infrastructure projects or long-term supply arrangements. Evaluate what kinds of activities in a joint venture would void or trigger unexpected obligations under guarantees of payment.

The best course of action is to meet with your foreign bankers as early in the process as possible to obtain their acquiescence to the proposed changes in the existing joint venture or to review how you expect to handle your financial arrangements.

Factor Seven: Customer Relationships

One major rationale for creating a joint venture between an American or European company and a Chinese company is to facilitate a good working relationship with local consumers through the contacts and presence of the Chinese partner. If a Chinese joint venture is dissolved or is expected to continue without the direct involvement of the local partner, you must place a high priority on maintaining existing customer relationships. Consider making personal visits to customers and/or facilities to occur simultaneously with any public announcement of a change in the structure or ownership of your joint venture.

Factor Eight: Foreign Distributors and Agents

It is common practice for foreign joint ventures to work with and through local agents and distributors as a way to heighten the effective penetration of markets. In many foreign countries, including

China, formal representative and distributor relationships may be registered with appropriate government authorities. In the event of reorganization, determine whether re-registration or reappointment of agents and/or distributors is required. A related question to resolve is whether dissolution of a joint venture will allow an agent or distributor to void ongoing obligations to the joint venture in the future.

ISSUE SIX

EXPATS VERSUS CHINESE EXECUTIVES IN YOUR CHINA OPERATIONS

When you decide to set up operations in China, either as part of a joint venture or a wholly owned subsidiary, one fundamental question that must be answered is whether to have a Chinese executive or a foreign expatriate run your Chinese operations. This is difficult for many American and European companies because they often desire to position their own executives into their China project. In my experience, it is nearly always better to use Chinese executives as opposed to expats. There are a number of reasons supporting this approach. First, though probably not the most important, is the language issue. Very few Westerners have the capability of speaking Mandarin and/or Cantonese at a level necessary to efficiently conduct operations without a full-time interpreter. Next, the cost of placing an expat in China is extremely high regardless of where the expat will be located. Finally, and most importantly, doing business in China requires an intimate understanding of Chinese culture, the Chinese people, and Chinese business practices. This kind of knowledge doesn't come from books and is best found in quality Chinese executives.

While twenty years ago it was difficult to find Chinese executives who had the capability to speak English, German, or French fluently, that has changed. With the growing economic might of China and opportunities emerging there, many Chinese who have lived and/or been educated overseas have returned to China. The best way to find these individuals is to work with a professional executive recruiter with specific expertise in China. One example is the executive search firm of Foster Partners, which is located in Shanghai and several other cities. As its president Trevor McCormick advises, "Do not make the mistake of thinking that you can hire high-quality Chinese executives for your operations inexpensively. As China's economy has exploded, so has the level of salaries that are commanded by the best executives." What headhunters in China most often do is go to other successful Chinese operations and lure away their executives to work for companies such as yours. You can expect to pay between 30% and 35% of the total first year's compensation to search firms in order to locate the best candidates in China. Finding the right people makes a good long-term investment.

One issue that comes up often and is little understood by European and American companies is how closely past relationship and historical factors influence China even today. For example, there are still strong feelings against the Japanese throughout China. During the 1930s and through the end of World War II, China suffered mightily at the hands of the Japanese militarists. Today, because of these historical conflicts, it still tends to be difficult for Japanese companies to do business and achieve success in China.

In short, the best of all worlds for your China operations would be to hire Chinese executives who are Western-educated or who have experience in working with American or European multinational companies.

Issue Seven

Tips on Negotiating in China

Entire books have been written on how to negotiate with the Chinese. What follows are some of the insights I have gained over twenty-five years. To begin, in my view, the Chinese are among the best negotiators in the world for one simple reason—they enjoy it. The Chinese approach to negotiations is much different from the Japanese. The Japanese in negotiations are always well prepared and very goal oriented, but ultimately they want to conclude negotiations in order to get on to the overall project. It has been my experience that the Chinese love the whole wheeling-and-dealing process and can and will extend negotiations if they find it in their best advantage.

There are some basics. Anyone who has ever negotiated in China knows that you never reveal in advance how long you expect the negotiation to take or when you plan to leave China to return home. Another is that the Chinese, for a strategic advantage, will spend a great deal of time dawdling over minor points, and then when time draws short will attempt to use the urgency as a strategy to extract concessions you might not otherwise want or be willing to give. The point is that in the absence of a very specific deadline, the Western concept of "time is of the essence" simply does not exist in China. The first and most important thing to remember is that negotiations in China will not follow a set schedule, no matter how hard you may try to establish one. This makes planning for negotiations much more difficult with the Chinese in that the time frame will rarely follow a strict pattern.

Perhaps the characteristic that most differentiates the Chinese from others is the flexibility that the Chinese exhibit during negotiations. Almost twenty years ago I participated in what was then known as a Chinese auction. I was negotiating on behalf of a U.S.-based manufacturer of sophisticated equipment used in the steel industry. Four companies were invited to China to bid on supplying one large piece of equipment, the enticement being that the winner of the bid could expect numerous follow-on sales to Chinese steel manufacturers. The four bidders were two Japanese companies, one American equipment manufacturer, and one German corporation. Each bidder was invited into a closed room for two hours to privately meet with the Chinese negotiating team. The Chinese asked each bidder to put on the table what machine it offered for sale, the spare parts that went with it, and the training and technology transfer that was part of the price. Over the first two days, each of the four parties was invited to make their bid. None of the four companies were told what the others had bid, but on the third day all were told that their price was "much too high" and to revise their bid. This process continued in this manner for almost three weeks until the German and one Japanese bidder pulled out. The two that remained, the American manufacturer and the other Japanese company, were once again invited into the room to bid. The American company finally refused to lower its bid yet again without being told what the Japanese company had offered. The Japanese company in the end won the bid at a great savings to the Chinese. The Chinese, by playing each bidder against the other, extracted great value with little effort aside from patience and guile.

In negotiating with the Chinese, you will commonly encounter six strategies:

1. *"Bigger Is Better."* The Chinese like to assemble sometimes unnecessarily large, somewhat intimidating negotiating teams. The teams are composed of individuals with strong technical backgrounds, financial expertise, and legal skills.
2. *"The Bait and Switch."* It is common for the Chinese not to identify a chief negotiator for their team, and then with little or no explanation replace the negotiator with another individual

when things do not necessarily go the way they had hoped. If possible, try to avoid this ploy, because it acts as a justification for renegotiating points that were already resolved. Tell the Chinese in the beginning that each party must agree to use the same lead negotiator throughout.

3. *"Time Is Timeless."* As described earlier, time is not of the essence when negotiating with the Chinese. They understand well the Western desire to "get the deal done," and so play off that with great skill and ingenuity.
4. *"Back to the Drawing Board."* I often recommend to my clients that before adjourning a negotiating session with the Chinese they summarize in writing what was agreed to that day. Then, the next morning before negotiations resume, read aloud from your list of what had been agreed to the prior day. Western negotiators often encounter the Chinese attempting to renegotiate what they believed had been already settled.
5. *"The Hidden Negotiator."* As described earlier in this chapter, the Chinese government is often involved, directly or indirectly, in commercial negotiations. This means you need to be savvy and think creatively about how to identify the real underlying motivations for the deal.
6. *"It's All or Nothing."* Western negotiators often like to gauge their level of success by working down a list of points they need to resolve in order to conclude a negotiation. This is where there are often significant misunderstandings between Western and Chinese negotiators. Western negotiators fail to understand that when the Chinese look at a contract, they view it as a whole rather than a series of individual parts. While the Chinese may agree to a point early on in a negotiation, if the negotiation nears an end and the Chinese perceive their earlier concession may be working against their interest, they will attempt to renegotiate that point or introduce a new issue. Recognize that this does not mean the Chinese are being disingenuous, rather that their concept of contracts is different than the Western view. While this complicates the process, it is important to appreciate it so a negotiation is not terminated

at an early stage because of a misunderstanding that can be easily dealt with.

When preparing for negotiations for a significant deal in China, I recommend that as in-house counsel you consider six key points when creating your own team strategy:

1. *Assemble Specialists and Resources.* Create your own team of specialists for a negotiation with the Chinese. You should mirror the Chinese team's levels of specializations, such as financial, commercial, accounting, and legal.
2. *Ignore Gender.* Gender is not an issue when negotiating with the Chinese. Many Chinese women hold high positions within the Chinese Communist Party, business enterprises, and society. You should not be surprised to come across a lead negotiator or senior individual on the Chinese negotiating team who is female. As a Western enterprise seeking business in China, you can consider using female negotiators or executives in the same way you would male.[1]
3. *Use a Primary Negotiator.* Designate your primary negotiator and consistently use him or her throughout the process. Do not switch negotiators, as this will enable you to force the Chinese to stick with their same negotiating team. This should help to accelerate the speed of negotiations.
4. *Keep Your CEO Away.* Do not include your top corporate executive or CEO as part of your negotiating team. Bring in a top executive only at the end of the negotiation, when a deal is ready to be signed. You need to maintain the ability when negotiating with the Chinese to see an impasse coming to "go back to the board" or "check with a senior executive" not present at the negotiation. It allows you to buy time if needed. If your chief executive is sitting in the room, you might find yourself forced to make an on-the-spot decision.
5. *Go Slowly.* For the reasons described earlier in this chapter, never try to artificially accelerate the negotiation process in China. The Chinese will resist this and might even attempt to extend the negotiations longer than otherwise needed.

6. *Be Very Prepared.* Be sure to carry out comprehensive, extensive preparations before your negotiations start and have a firm grasp of all of the commercial, legal, and financial aspects involved. The Chinese will be extremely well prepared, and in order to be successful you need to mirror their level of preparation.

ISSUE EIGHT
HOW THE CHINESE VIEW INTELLECTUAL PROPERTY

The Chinese view intellectual property with skepticism, and this is a challenge. The reason is that the protection of intellectual property, which is so well embraced in the West, is generally not accepted on a philosophical level in China and elsewhere in Asia.

The Chinese have trouble accepting the fundamental premise that a single company or individual with a valuable patent or piece of intellectual property should have the right to protect it to the point of it not being generally available. An example of this is in the case when a pharmaceutical, chemical formulation, or mechanical process is at stake, and this protected technology could have widespread use and benefit. The Chinese may object if the intellectual property is of a nature that would allow the Chinese economy to expand. These attitudes are behind why the Chinese are reluctant to protect intellectual property. It isn't that their intention is to steal intellectual property; it is just that they feel it is unreasonable for the owners to artificially exploit them.

After joining the World Trade Organization, (WTO), China was forced to adopt new ways of strengthening its intellectual property laws for both Chinese companies and foreign investors in China. Unfortunately, changing the laws and attitudes of Chinese courts toward intellectual property remains a long-term process.

One major factor which I think will ultimately alter the views of the Chinese in the long run is the rapid internationalization of Chinese companies. For example, the Chinese company Lenovo years ago was a hardware manufacturer and outsourcer for IBM computers. Lenovo, as most readers already know, purchased the personal computer business from IBM several years ago. As a result, Lenovo now has its own intellectual property and trademarks. This same trend occurred in Taiwan in the early 1980s, when there was little research being done in Taiwan and Taiwanese companies were known for intellectual property theft. This changed over the last twenty years, and so now a lot of research and development goes on in Taiwan; as a result, the intellectual property regime there is much stronger than it was in the past.

In brief, do not expect intellectual property protection to be as enforceable in China as it would be in Europe or the United States. As in-house counsel, you have to carefully judge on an ongoing basis what kinds of technologies will be licensed, sold, or used in China and then do a cost-benefit analysis of what happens if those intellectual property rights are infringed upon by the Chinese in one way or the other. In the long run, intellectual property protection will become strengthened in China, but it is an issue that deserves close and ongoing attention.

Issue Nine

The Chinese Courts, Legal System, and Arbitration

The fundamental difference between the court system in the United States and many parts of Europe and China is that there is no distinct separation between the judicial system and executive decision making. This means that courts in China may reflect political decisions made by the central government or provincial leaders. For example, Chinese courts in the past have been more or less responsive to foreign complaints about intellectual property, depending on how important that issue was to the central government in Beijing.

On the most basic levels, as in-house counsel you must accept the fact that under Chinese law, if you as a non-Chinese investor have a joint venture or a wholly owned subsidiary in China, you will in most cases find yourself under the jurisdiction of Chinese courts.

China has adopted a system of arbitration referred to as CIETAC arbitration. There are CIETAC arbitration tribunals in Beijing, Shanghai, and Shenzhen. It is common for foreign investors in China to find themselves subject to either Chinese courts or CIETAC arbitration. Although there are advantages and disadvantages to both, in my experience, most foreign investors tend to opt for arbitration over Chinese courts when it comes to dispute resolution.

Issue Ten

Identifying, Hiring, and Managing Legal Counsel in China

Until the early 1990s, there were essentially no independent lawyers or law firms in China. The law firms that did exist were closely tied to the Chinese government. That has changed greatly over the last decade as independent Chinese law firms have sprung up throughout the country. Although the Chinese were very slow to permit foreign law firms to set up operations in China, that situation has now slowly begun to evolve.

One trend I see is that as Chinese enterprises become larger, they are seeking on a more frequent basis Chinese law firms that are manned by Chinese lawyers for both their domestic and international activities. At first, major Chinese companies flocked to foreign law firms, which were often in joint ventures with local law firms, to provide legal advice.

I strongly recommend that all in-house counsel needing to hire outside lawyers for a significant transaction personally go to China and directly interview on a face-to-face basis several Chinese law firms before deciding which to select.

Conclusion

Despite its progress, China will face three major challenges over the next decade.

Challenge One: Rich China/Poor China

The major challenge that I see China facing over the next twenty to thirty years is what I call "Rich China/Poor China." China is not a single country from an economic standpoint. It has vast economic and geographic diversity. While parts of China are booming, others are suffering significant challenges that will continue into the future. If you look at a map of China and draw a line down the coastline from the city of Shenyang north of Beijing all the way south of Hong Kong and Macao and go inland about 100 miles, you have an area with a population of about 450 million people. Those 450 million people are exceptionally wealthy compared to the rest of China. The reason is that when China began establishing its special economic zones in the early 1980s, the first was set up in the Pearl River Delta region, which has about 90 million people. Because of special tax incentives and government deals, this area developed first and became the export capital and center of all of China. It benefited from the fact that one of the world's great ports exists in Hong Kong, and the products that were made there could be shipped out around the world. Next, there was great economic development in the area around Fuzhou and Xiamen. A lot of the investment that went into that part of China originated in Taiwan and was invested through indirect sources. After that, Shanghai boomed. Greater Shanghai now has around 35 million people in what one day may be the major financial center of China, and perhaps the world. Currently, Beijing and its port Tianjin are experiencing massive growth. When you group together these coastline regions, you have what is best known as Rich China. The income along the coast is on the average three to four times as high as it is through the rest of China.

The problem the Chinese government faces is the rest of China, which goes from far in the north near Harbin to the west near Urumqi to the south near Kunming. This vast area is home to about 900 million Chinese. With the majority of China being largely agricultural, and the attraction of the wealth along the coast, we are seeing what is potentially the largest migration of people in the history of the world moving from rural areas toward the cities.

Obviously, the Chinese government cannot allow this to happen unchecked; otherwise the cities will be overrun with people they cannot support.

To combat this, the Chinese government has attempted to develop industries and infrastructure in the central part of the country in cities like Wuhan and Chengdu. While the Chinese government has been partially successful so far, there continues to be enormous pressure, particularly from the young people, to move from the agricultural areas to the urbanized parts of China. This is the one issue that on a macro level China has to effectively address if it expects to continue the growth it has experienced over the last thirty years.

Challenge Two: Infrastructure

Over the last thirty years, China has undergone one of the great building projects in the history of the world. It has built thousands of miles of roads, railroads, and pipelines. The Three River Gorges project is just one example of how China has attempted to recreate its basic geography in order to benefit the Chinese people. The problem is that the infrastructure developments are again along the coast and not as much within the country. It still remains very difficult to move people and goods from the central part of China to the coast where they can either be consumed or exported.

One of the major infrastructure challenges comes in the field of energy. To support both industry and the increasing demands of the Chinese populace, China has no choice but to undertake massive power station building. In the last year, it has ordered from Westinghouse four large nuclear plants, which are to go into operation in 2016. But China probably needs at least another twenty plants in the next ten years, plus other more traditional forms of energy generation. The problem with the traditional generation of energy through burning of coal is that it adds to China's already serious environmental problems. While China can deal with these challenges, it needs to devote significant resources, and to date it has not done so.

You begin to see now strong pressures within China itself to create a more environmentally acceptable climate. The health costs of having unchecked pollution is causing the kinds of serious health problems which again China has to deal with on a nationwide basis.

Challenge Three: Looking In and Looking Out

China has been the beneficiary of direct foreign investment that has amounted to well over $1 trillion over the last thirty years. Because of foreign investment, China has managed to achieve an annual growth rate of between 9% and 12%. One of the problems is that China now faces pressures from its trading partners in Europe, the United States, and elsewhere to recirculate many of the dollars and hard currencies that have accumulated. China has in the last several years adopted a new law that more closely looks at inbound investment into China. It is unclear at this point whether China will continue to embrace foreign inbound investment as it has in the past.

A related problem for China is its currency. The renminbi (or yuan) is not a freely or openly convertible currency. The Chinese have tagged the renminbi to the U.S. dollar. The advantage of doing this is that China has kept the cost of its labor artificially low, which has benefited its export industries. It is those Chinese export industries, though, that were most seriously hurt in 2008 and 2009 during the recession. While China is under tremendous pressures to let the renminbi float, it is reluctant to do so because of the political consequences. China has promised to relieve its stance, but only time will tell what will happen.

China today is a dominant, strong economic power in the world. A psychological problem it faces is that it now has to begin to act like a major world power, which means it cannot protect its industries and follow policies that harm its image around the world. The challenge here is that China must begin to coordinate its economic policy along with its political presence in the world. If it does not do this in the most appropriate way, China may face strong protectionist backlash from many countries in the West. If that kind of protectionism arises, then China as well as those other countries in the West would be badly harmed.

CHAPTER SIX

KOREA: ONE PEOPLE, TWO NATIONS

The Korean Peninsula was always a strategic prize for those seeking control of the sea lanes along the Western Pacific. The Chinese, Mongolians, and Japanese have each forcibly subjugated the Korean people at one time. This sad history ended after World War II, but by then what became North Korea and South Korea were counted among the poorest nations in the world, with no natural resources and barely enough food to feed themselves. In time, the South prospered; the North did not. The North remains isolated and a rogue internationally. Years spent rebuilding, establishing a national identity, and recovering from the never-ending threat of foreign invasion molded the South Koreans into a nation of fiercely independent and proud people. Doing business in South Korea—and expecting to succeed—demands a comprehensive understanding of Korea's background, culture, and needs.

Understanding Koreans

To truly understand Korean culture, you must begin by looking back a very, very long time. The country is ancient. Archaeologists have discovered pottery on the Korean Peninsula more than 8,000 years old. Like China, Korea followed an evolutionary path from a Neolithic to a bronze to an iron-based culture.

Underlying tensions that emanate throughout the Korean peninsula have their genesis in historical events. Specifically, those living on the Korean Peninsula have faced constant challenges throughout history because of Korea's strategic geographic position in Asia. During the late 1600s, Japan invaded Korea for perhaps the first (but not the last) time. In the 17th century, China was ruled by the Manchu Qing Dynasty, which tried to incorporate the Korean Peninsula by force. China was ultimately not successful in conquering Korea, but its influence over modern-day Korean culture is extensive.

The Meiji Restoration began in Japan in the 1860s, and during this period Japan became increasingly militaristic. One aspect of Japan's military endeavors included a sustained campaign to squeeze the Chinese out of the Korean Peninsula. After an Empress in Korea was assassinated in 1895, the Korean Peninsula officially became known for the first time as Korea, or the Korean Empire.

Japan officially annexed Korea in 1905, forcing Korea to become its protectorate. Five years later, Korea technically became part of Japan. The Koreans were wholly subsumed by the Japanese until Japan surrendered in Tokyo Bay in 1945. As World War II ended, Korea found itself one of the poorest regions on earth. Under the United Nations, Korea was divided into two separate countries (North Korea and South Korea). The UN-designated separation of North and South Korea became permanent following the conclusion of the Korean War in 1953.

My point in outlining Korea's history is to make you aware that the Korean people (both North and South) have a long, sad record of being overrun and controlled directly and indirectly by foreign powers. An understanding of their history and how they have had to fight strongly against outsiders is essential if you expect to negotiate with the Koreans. You will find that Koreans are an extremely proud people who have developed a natural aggressiveness in response to the challenges they have confronted over the years. Not surprisingly, the Koreans have a deep-seated aversion to both the Japanese and the Chinese based on historical interactions. The Koreans may be willing to work with outsiders, but it would probably be futile to attempt to forge a three-part joint venture among an American, a Korean, and a Japanese or Chinese company.

At the time of the writing of this book, American companies and individuals are generally prohibited from doing business with North Korea pursuant to sanction laws and embargo programs enforced by the U.S. Treasury Department's Office of Foreign Assets Control (OFAC). Consequently, all subsequent references to Korea in this chapter shall refer to the Republic of Korea, better known as South Korea.

THE *CHAEBOLS* OF SOUTH KOREA

This book's chapter on Japan describes of the powerful military/ industrial groups that were once known as the *zaibatsu* and evolved into the *keiretsu* after World War II. Just as the *keiretsu* have contributed to the power of Japan and its economy, the *chaebols* have similarly impacted life in Korea with certain, distinct differences.

For two decades following the Korean War, South Korea remained an extremely poor nation. South Korea's ability to forge a strong economy resulted from the unique and symbiotic relationship that existed between the Korean government and the country's family-owned businesses. The single most powerful political leader in Korea during the 20th century, Park Chung Hee, encouraged this trend. Park ran Korea with an iron fist. When he first came into power, Park realized that something radical had to be done in order for Korea to advance to a modern economy. Looking to Japan as an example, Park tied what were originally family-owned firms in Korea to the Korean government. These industrial groups came to be known as the *chaebols*. Like Japan, Korea allocated its limited resources to key industries that were seen as essential to jump-starting its economy. While the *keiretsu* in Japan relied on banks or financial institutions within each *keiretsu*, the *chaebols* received their money directly from the Korean government because Park nationalized the Korean banks in the 1960s. Consequently, the *chaebols* were able to grow rapidly and become extremely powerful because they essentially had access to unlimited sources of funds. Nevertheless, size and power did not guarantee the profitability of the *chaebols*. For example, during the 1997 financial crisis in Asia, the Korean economy would have totally failed but for the direct intervention of the International Monetary Fund (IMF) and Korea's political allies such as the United States.

Some *chaebols* have existed for fifty years and remain powerful to this day, including Lucky Gold Star (LG). Samsung is another example of a *chaebol* that is not only large, but has grown into a world-class international competitor. Other *chaebols* have risen to prominence more recently, such as Hyundai Motors, which was a direct beneficiary of the preferential lending directed to the Hyundai *chaebol* through the auspices of the Korean government. Additional examples of large, modern *chaebols* in Korea are Daewoo, Sangyong, Lotte, and Hanjin.

Some mid-sized Korean firms have begun to emerge in recent years, but the *chaebols* remain immensely powerful within the

Korean economy. You will find it is difficult to do business to any significant degree in Korea without involving one or more of the *chaebols*. While the importance of the *keiretsu* in Japan has declined over time, the *chaebols* still exercise enormous economic influence within Korea.

FOREIGN DIRECT INVESTMENT AND THE ROLE OF THE KOREAN GOVERNMENT

Any foreign investor interested in doing business in Korea must realize that the Korean government will take an active role in regulating and approving (or disapproving) any proposed investment. While the Korean government probably will not prohibit a foreign investment entirely, an American investor will discover that it is quite challenging to have an investment approved by the Korean government, at least initially. The Koreans are far more aggressive in regulating investments than the Japanese.

Korea's Foreign Investment Promotion Act (FIPA) is the fundamental statute that regulates commercial joint ventures between foreign investors and local Korean firms. FIPA sets forth minimum foreign capitalization levels (as of this writing, about 50 million Won (KRW)) and the percentage interest that must be held by a foreign partner. There is a multiplicity of filing requirements in Korea, whether a foreign company wishes to directly invest in a Korean business or whether the foreign company has entered into certain kinds of contracts with a Korean party. The Koreans view certain types of contracts as foreign investments, such as if a contract requires a supply of raw materials or the purchase of products for at least a year, provides for joint research and development or importing of certain foreign technologies, or appoints a foreign individual to carry out certain business activities for a Korean corporation.

Advice: An investor needs to have a solid understanding of the role played by the Korean government both during the investment stage and afterward before making a significant commitment to do business in Korea. This generalization is not to suggest the Korean government is opposed to foreign investment, but for national policy purposes it likes to ensure that any proposed foreign investment is in line with what the Korean Ministry of Strategy and Finance (MSF) or the Ministry of Knowledge and Economy (MKE) decide are good for Korea. In addition, it is helpful to retain on-the-ground Korean advisors who are politically connected and will work with you during the preliminary stages of an investment. I have found that experienced Korean lawyers can be very helpful in the process because they have a good understanding of the relationship between the Korean government and major corporations. In addition, the Korean lawyer's contacts can be invaluable.

Terminating Agents and Distributors in Korea

It is common for Western companies to retain one or more agents in the foreign countries in which they conduct business. Appointment of such an agent may be exclusive or nonexclusive. In either case, circumstances can arise when it becomes evident that the foreign agent is the wrong person for the job, which is not always a matter of incompetence or lack of effort. While a foreign agent may be extremely competent at sales, the ability to develop the right business contacts or relationships is often more important. South Korea is a highly homogenous and competitive society and provides a good example of this principle. While it may be an exaggeration to say that everyone in Korea knows everyone else, the country is small enough (less than half of Japan's population and less than 5% of China's population) that in the business world, most of the players know each other or at least know about each other. Consequently, an effective agent in Korea must be well connected.

If your company needs to replace its existing Korean agent, you may have a problem because the relationship with your Korean agent is not necessary governed by the agent or representative contract agreed to by both parties. The Korean Civil Code and the Korean Commercial Code (KCC) are the key to consider because they outline in detail the rights, duties, and obligations of both parties to an agency contract. Remember—the Code trumps an agency contract if the two come into conflict.

You can expect that a terminated Korean agent will make a claim for money damages (i.e., compensation) under the KCC. You will find this type of claim is similar to what terminated agents in other countries such as Malaysia, Thailand, and Indonesia can assert. The KCC is vague as to termination, but a terminated agent may request that his former employer pay the average yearly compensation he received for up to five years before the agency contract ends. The terminated agent must show that the employer will continue to receive income from business he recruited on its behalf. Of course, the agent will likely also claim that he was terminated for reasons other than his own performance, and the former employer will have to rebut this assertion before a Korean tribunal. In Korea, as in most countries in Asia, the foreign company faces an uphill battle regardless of the factual basis for termination.

As for distributor contracts in South Korea, it is not clear whether the same principles outlined in the Korean Commercial Code (KCC) that apply to agents also apply to distributors. In my experience, distributor contracts are less protected and may be easier to enforce (i.e., terminate) based upon their terms. Nevertheless, an unhappy Korean distributor will look to the KCC for relief.

Advice: Before your company signs any agency or distributor contracts in South Korea, check first with an experienced Korean business attorney. What you need is not just a pro forma contract but, more importantly, practical advice from the Korean attorney as to what you can expect if termination results. Obviously, if you encounter a problem with an existing contract in Korea (agency or distributor), say nothing to your agent or distributor until after you have reviewed all of the facts with Korean counsel. Employment termination is not an area in which your businesspeople can do a "handshake" settlement. Document the termination well, or it will come back to haunt you later.

Contracts in Korea

As a Westerner, do not assume that a contract in South Korea has the same meaning for the Koreans as it does for you. The idea of a binding commercial contract that contains all details of the relationship between two or more parties within its pages is not the Korean way. South Koreans will always look at a contract as a flexible document not to be strictly construed. If and when an event arises that was not anticipated by the parties, or one that would put the Korean party in a disadvantageous position, you can assume that the Koreans will expect to renegotiate or open discussions on the contract. They do not strive to be disingenuous; it is simply the Korean view. Remember that the relationship between individuals in Korea is extremely important. Extending that concept, it is reasonable for the Koreans to believe that if two parties enter into a contract that subsequently becomes difficult for one of the parties to perform, then the two "good friends" need to sit down together and discuss it. This generalization is not to suggest that major corporations like Hyundai and Samsung would not respect and follow commercial contracts, but it is important to note that you will have to be much more flexible in dealing with the Koreans down the road than you would be in the case of a commercial contract with the Japanese.

Negotiating with the Koreans

There are four words you should never say during a Korean negotiation: "That is not fair." The Koreans are among the finest and most aggressive negotiators in the world. If you make a misstep or are seeking an accommodation from your Korean counterpart, forget it. The concept of "fair" never plays a part in any negotiation in Korea.

However, it is true that Koreans will first desire to form a relationship with you before substantive negotiations may begin. For example, if you travel to Korea for initial discussions and the Koreans do not have their lawyers and senior business advisors present in the room or even close by, you can relax. No serious business will be conducted that day because they are simply taking the first step in a long process of getting to know you. The Koreans will not start until they are ready.

Nevertheless, once serious negotiations begin, all bets are off. You have to assume that the Koreans will be absolutely prepared to push forward. It is a certainty that their negotiating team was handpicked very carefully. If someone has a spot on the team, that individual is there for a specific purpose. The Koreans leave nothing to chance. For example, if a member of the Korean team is more than sixty years old, he is probably there as a "father figure" whose role is to settle disputes. He will look to interact with the oldest member of your team or, as is often the case, will be the one delegated to communicate with senior executives in your home office if negotiations go off track. Watch for younger members on the Korean team who may not appear to speak English. You will often find that they speak perfect English and have completed a postgraduate program in Europe or the United States. These team members will be the ones most culturally aware of Western attitudes and ideas, but will not show it publicly.

Again, nothing is left to chance. The Korean team is structured like an army with a general at the top, a colonel, lieutenants, and soldiers. While who is who is not supposed to be obvious to outsiders, each team member knows his role. If something unexpected happens during negotiations, such as a brutal verbal exchange instigated by a Korean party, you can assume it did not happen by chance. The Koreans may carefully plan such an incident to provoke a specific reaction from your team. My advice when this happens is not to react in any way. Simply call an end to the negotiations for the day and walk out of the room. When the Koreans try to apologize for their actions, politely smile, say nothing, and leave. They will get the point and this tactic will not be used again. If you stay in the room, you have lost.

Patience is the one characteristic you cannot do without when negotiating in Korea. Declaring a deadline is a guarantee that your schedule will fail. Expect to bargain long and hard to reach an agreement. Some American negotiators try to shorten the process by saying something like, "Here is the bottom line that we need to do this deal." Never say that, even if it happens to be true. The Koreans will simply not believe you, because no one in Korea would ever say such a thing, and they will think it is just a ploy.

Advice: The Koreans would make Machiavelli proud. They are wonderful negotiators who leave nothing to chance. Be prepared for anything, and *never* react emotionally. Expect to be baited. When unsure, adjourn negotiations and take the rest of the day off. An experienced Korean lawyer can be a big help. Before concluding your negotiation, remember that signing a contract in Korea is just the beginning. Koreans will constantly try to renegotiate the terms of your contract as time goes on, as is their nature. Remember, if you had been colonized and overrun by outsiders for thousands of years, you would probably react much the same way.

Korean Courts and Arbitration

There are no juries in Korea. Like Japan, Korea has no American-style discovery in litigation. Judges are fact finders and decision makers on all Korean legal issues.

As a general rule, it is difficult to enforce a foreign judgment in Korea. There are many procedural hurdles a foreigner must overcome in seeking to have a judgment from another jurisdiction enforced, and a favorable outcome is far from certain. Frankly, I would not waste my time trying.

Commercial disputes in the Korean court system are resolved by a panel of three judges. The reality though is that most commercial disputes between Korean and foreign parties are reached through arbitration, not in Korean courts. Before adding an arbitration clause to your contracts with a Korean party, take a close look at the Korean Arbitration Act. Carefully research how this act works before electing where and how to arbitrate.

Practical Business Advice for Korea

What follows are eight commonsense suggestions when conducting business in Korea.

1. *Dress.* Even more so than in Japan, you will find that formal dress in Korea is expected. For men, a dark suit, white shirt, and conservative tie are always correct, and women should dress accordingly. Never "dress down" unless you are perhaps going to the golf course with your Korean hosts.
2. *Attitude.* Koreans can appear confusing to outsiders because they are very aggressive and outgoing during negotiations and then extremely private on a one-to-one basis. Underneath their public persona, you will discover that most Koreans expect you to be comparably humble and modest in your dealings with them. It is much better as a non-Korean to be quiet in manner and approach and reciprocate in a stronger sense only if that is how you are asked to respond. Braggarts should stay at home! The worst thing you can do is talk yourself up by explaining how many "big" deals you have done or how many people work for you. Your Korean counterpart will have done a background check on you in advance, so talking about yourself is unnecessary and viewed as inappropriate unless asked.
3. *Timing.* Korean people are extremely punctual and not only expect the same timeliness from their foreign business partners but consider it an insult if someone is late. If for some reason you cannot arrive at a meeting when scheduled, be sure to give your Korean counterpart as much advance notice as possible. Failure to do so will be viewed as a personal affront and will damage the chances for creating a beneficial relationship.
4. *Business Cards.* The Japanese and Koreans share similar views regarding business cards. When traveling to Korea, you should have at least your name, if not all of your contact information, printed in the Korean language on the opposite side of your business card. When you present the card to someone in Korea for the first time, use two hands. When you receive someone else's card, also take it with two hands and study it carefully. Ask your counterpart how to pronounce his name, explain the exact title of the job, and describe what he does. Taking the time to admire the card and then ask questions shows in a genuine sense that the person is important to you.

Most experienced executives in Asia, particularly in Japan and Korea, have a special card carrying case. Never just take someone's business card, put it in your wallet, and return your wallet to your back pocket. After commenting on the card, place it in a carrying case in an honored spot.

5. *Personal Relationship.* More so than in Japan or China, creating a personal relationship in Korea is key to a successful negotiation. If your Korean counterpart is not comfortable with you as a person, then your anticipated business relationship is unlikely to come to fruition. I strongly suggest dinners with your Korean counterpart, which provide an easy atmosphere for bonding and sampling local delicacies. While an outsider is not expected to eat all types of Korean food (which is excellent), you should at least express an interest in sampling. As in most other cultures, unwillingness to even try the regional cuisine is a serious misstep.
6. *Gifts.* Giving gifts in Korea, as in most Asian countries, is a confusing process. When in doubt, it is better not to give a gift unless you are reciprocating in kind to a gift you have received. The worst thing you can do is give a gift that is "over the top," because the recipient will feel embarrassed if he or she cannot present you with something of equal or greater value.
7. *Use of Names.* When in doubt, always address someone as "Mr. X," "Mrs. X," or "Miss X." As in China, Korean last names are printed first followed by what would be considered a first name in the West. Many Americans err by being too friendly initially and trying to create a relationship by using someone's first name. Never use the first name of a Korean with whom you are doing business unless he or she specifically asks you to do so.
8. *Face.* It is easy to create a loss of face without even knowing it. You should never, under any circumstances, publicly criticize someone in Korea. Open criticism is most inappropriate in Korean society, as is speaking too loudly or gesturing in a wild and effusive manner.

CHAPTER SEVEN

THE PHILIPPINES: SOMEWHERE BETWEEN EAST AND WEST

A friend of mine who managed a factory in the Philippines contracted to have some work done during a renovation project. At one point, the Filipino contractor came by with a package containing $20,000 in cash that was being returned as a "gift." The factory manager refused, saying he did not require this kickback as the work was done well and was bid at a competitive price—no bribe was part of the deal. The contractor persisted, saying, "This is how it is done here; please accept." The factory manager again refused, and the contractor left. Once the factory renovations were complete, the manager flew back to the United States.

Three months later, a crate arrived at the manager's office. Inside the crate were four framed watercolors (of no commercial value) that the manager had admired on the wall of a small four-table Philippine café while having lunch with the contractor eight months earlier. The accompanying note said only, "I remember that you liked these. Please accept a gesture of friendship." It was then clear to the manager that while the bribe was refused, the contractor still wanted to show a personal connection and a unique demonstration of their relationship. The money was not the crucial point; the friendship was.

For some reason, when most people think about the countries of Asia, the Philippines rarely comes to mind. This is surprising, because the Philippines is the twelfth-largest country in the world by population and plays a significant role in the economics of Southeast Asia. Located midway between Taiwan and Vietnam and in close proximity to China, the Philippines is a culturally diverse nation. In addition, the Philippines shares many common characteristics with Western countries, far more so than most other countries in Asia, which makes the country truly one of a kind.

There are two official languages in the Philippines—Filipino (Tagalog) and English—as well as about a dozen other regional dialects. Other languages commonly heard throughout parts of the Philippines are Arabic and Spanish, whose roots go back to the country's colonial past.

The strategic value of the Philippines was recognized by countries with colonial aspirations as far back as Ferdinand Magellan in the 16th century. At the time, the Spanish were among the most successful of trading nations and were quick to recognize the key geographic position of the Philippines. The country was strategically located in the middle of the trade routes connecting the East with Europe's burgeoning merchant middle class. Ships under the Spanish flag also frequently sailed across the Pacific to Acapulco, filled with trade goods. Economic incentives are a key factor in understanding why the Spanish forcibly colonized the Philippines for more than 300 years, until the early 20th century when Spanish rule was replaced by the United States.

Following bloody battles between Japanese troops and U.S. forces during World War II, the Philippines gained independence as a country for the first time in 400 years. Although there were previous periods of strained political relations between the U.S. and Philippine governments over sovereignty issues (such as extensions on the leases for the Clark Air Force Base and Subic Bay), close cultural and political ties now exist between the two countries.

Because the Philippines contains such a unique mix of Eastern and Western characteristics, local knowledge is absolutely essential if you expect to succeed in conducting business there. It is a mistake to try to apply strategies employed elsewhere in Asia to business negotiations in the Philippines. This chapter describes some successful techniques for foreign companies contemplating transactions with Philippine entities.

HOW THE PHILIPPINE GOVERNMENT FUNCTIONS

When trying to understand how business is conducted in the Philippines, a good place to start is by looking at the structure of the Philippine government. Although the Philippine form of government appears very Western at first glance, it is in fact a form of democracy known as a unitary presidential constitutional republic. Under this system, the president of the Philippines, who is elected for a six-year term, is extremely powerful, particularly as compared to the leaders of Western nations. The president serves not just as the nation's chief executive but also as its head of state and commander in chief of the military forces. In addition, the president does not need to consult with anyone when appointing his or her cabinet. The Philippine court system is also not independent (as is often the case in the West), because the president of the Philippines appoints the chief justice along with the fourteen Justices of the Supreme Court. Though the Philippines has a bicameral legislature, the president remains the most powerful political figure in the country. Opposition movements in the past have tried (and failed) to introduce a parliamentary or federal system of government. Overall, the government's structure enables the president to control the country with wide latitude and few real checks and balances.

The Long Shadow of the Marcos Regime

Ferdinand Marcos was one of the most iconic and flawed political figures of the 20th century. During the long period of Marcos's rule in the Philippines from the 1960s to the 1980s, the country suffered from massive internal abuses and widespread institutional corruption. Although the sad legacy of the Marcos regime is now in the past, there are interestingly still some citizens in the Philippines who would like to see a return to the Marcos form of government. To be fair, the Marcos regime did achieve certain positive developments. Marcos was, to the surprise of many, instrumental in attracting significant foreign investment to the Philippines, which led to economic growth benefiting most levels of Philippine society, even the bottom. Prior to Marcos, few foreign investors looked seriously at the Philippines as a potential place to do business. As a strong anti-Communist with the open backing of the U.S. government and the Catholic Church (at least at first), Marcos was able to stay in power for a long time.

One result of the Marcos legacy is that moral challenges still exist in the Philippines, as in other countries throughout Asia. While the current regime has been successful in suppressing certain corrupt tendencies, as legal counsel you need to be cognizant of the country's checkered history when conducting business in the Philippines.

COURTS VERSUS ARBITRATION FOR DISPUTE RESOLUTION

Historically, the court system in the Philippines has been politically influenced because of the power of the president to appoint the members of the Supreme Court as well as lower-level members of the judiciary. The politicization of the Philippine judiciary concerned many outside investors in the past and continues to influence their decisions regarding choice of law provisions today. As a result, in most commercial contracts of significant size, arbitration is the preferred form of dispute resolution. Philippine courts recognize the role of arbitrators and are unlikely to set aside a final decision by an arbitral panel. If you elect arbitration to govern in the event a dispute arises under a Philippine contract, the decision of the arbitrators will be recognized.

Another factor to consider in deciding whether to provide for arbitration or dispute resolution by the Philippine courts is the country's widespread public press, which publishes all kinds of information, often in a tabloid setting. Traditionally, multinational corporations have been portrayed unfavorably in the Philippine press because of past allegations involving corruption. This threat of unwanted notoriety has increased foreign companies' interest in arbitration as opposed to courts because arbitral proceedings are confidential. Arbitration makes it possible for multinational corporations to keep their disputes in the Philippines out of the public eye.

One final aspect of arbitration in the Philippines that appeals to multinational corporations is the ability to select an arbitrator or arbitrators who possess a specific type of expertise. Multinational corporations often decide to go with arbitration because of the ability to design specific clauses governing the selection and classification of arbitrators. Unless there is some specific business reason that would argue otherwise, I always strongly recommend using arbitration in the Philippines for commercial contracts of any major size.

CAUTION

On a one-on-one basis, no people in Asia are more genuinely open to outsiders than the Filipinos. You will feel welcomed and accepted every time you visit. Unfortunately, though, street crime—a vestige of the Marcos era—still exists not only in the countryside but also in the Philippines' largest cities, including Manila. Your personal safety and that of your clients can never be taken for granted in the Philippines; foreigners must be cognizant of their surroundings at all times.

Technology and Intellectual Property Protection in the Philippines

The Philippines, like most other countries in Asia, has adopted a wide range of laws designed to protect patents, trademarks, and copyrights. To this end, the Philippine government has also ratified most of the major international intellectual property conventions. Philippine courts will generally support legitimate claims filed by intellectual property owners. The protection of intellectual property is guaranteed in the Philippine constitution.

Filipinos are highly literate, and English is their first language for business. Consequently, a significant number of foreign investors—including many from the United States—have been attracted to the Philippines to set up back-office operations and call centers. One practical reason for this choice is that the Filipino form of English, to the American ear, is accented more like Spanish than accents used by phone operators at call centers in other parts of the world, such as India. Companies using call centers in the Philippines have found the level of acceptance by U.S.-based customers to be higher than the satisfaction rate at other foreign locations. Another major advantage of using the Philippines is that Filipinos tend to understand American approaches to doing business, and most are acquainted with U.S.-based accounting methods.

A product of the Philippines' quality educational system is that Filipinos are very adept at writing software and code. This is a double-edged sword though, in that the country is recognized as a hub for computer hackers and viruses. If a foreign company decides to set up technology operations in the Philippines, its personnel must be extremely vigilant first in hiring trustworthy employees and later in ensuring that its networks are secure from unwanted attention and cyber-attacks. Certainly the Philippines is not the only country in Asia with computer hacking problems, but the higher incidence here makes it is a concern worth exploring.

INSIGHTS INTO THE FILIPINOS

Without a doubt, the Filipinos are some of the warmest and most open people you will encounter anywhere in Asia. You should naturally find yourself very comfortable dealing with them. Culturally, Filipinos are more like Spaniards or Brazilians than they are like other Asians, partially as a result of Spain's colonization of the Philippines for more than three centuries. Surprisingly, the Filipino openness to outsiders prevails over any remnants of anticolonial bias. The Filipinos seem to sincerely appreciate the income opportunities that foreign investments offer and have been able to get past the memories of being forcibly colonized when dealing with outsiders.

Another interesting aspect of Filipino culture is the role of religion in the citizens' everyday lives. More than 80 percent of Filipinos are followers of the Roman Catholic Church, and between 10 and 15 percent of the remaining population is Muslim. The role of the Catholic Church has been omnipresent in influencing Filipino thinking for centuries, and the Church has significant sway in political and economic issues. Therefore, when you are visiting the Philippines, my advice is, *never discuss religion.* Specifically, inquiring about or criticizing the role of the Catholic Church in the Philippines will only lead to problems.

SUBIC BAY

Subic Bay is an example of how a carefully structured foreign investment plan can succeed. The U.S. Navy occupied the Subic Bay Military Base from the end of World War II until its lease expired in 1992, at which point the Philippine government decided to redirect

Subic Bay as a target destination for foreign investors. The former military base is now known as the Subic Bay Freeport Zone.

Today more than 600 companies are based in Subic Bay and the nearby Clark Freeport Zone (formerly the Clark Air Force Base). One of the major attractions is the natural port that was first used by the Spanish 350 years ago. In addition to the deep-water port, Subic Bay is an attractive place for foreign investors because it has reliable power, good water resources, airport facilities, well-qualified workers, and very low levels of corruption. Doing business throughout Asia is easy from Subic Bay because of its excellent infrastructure and close proximity to other countries.

The Philippine government offers two levels of incentives to foreign companies interested in Subic Bay, including classification as a Subic Bay Regional Enterprise, which can qualify for certain tax benefits. If you are considering doing business in the Philippines and do not want or need a location near Manila, it is worth analyzing Subic Bay as a possible location.

How Filipinos View Commercial Contracts

The Philippine view of contracts is much like in the West, meaning once a contract is negotiated and its terms are agreed upon, Filipinos will generally adhere to the terms of the contract. Filipinos will resist the urge to constantly renegotiate, unlike their counterparts in Korea or China, where renegotiation after the fact is always expected.

As has been mentioned throughout this chapter, the Filipinos are extremely open and optimistic about life and its prospects. In negotiations, you will find the Filipinos will always work hard to create a positive outcome. The downside of this cultural optimism is that sometimes you may find yourself in a situation where the Filipinos promise too much in a contract. Though a Filipino business has the sincerest intention to perform, a Filipino partner may get in over his or her head by promising too much or agreeing to too short a time frame that cannot realistically be met. The problem may be exacerbated because the Filipinos are reluctant to admit when they are going to fall short in their performance obligations and will instead try to compensate. Consequently, I recommend that if a foreign party enters into a significant contract in the Philippines, it must constantly monitor the performance of his partner and be prepared to jump in at any point to confirm that things are going according to plan. Do not expect a heads-up from your Filipino partner if something goes wrong. One method used by a friend of mine who works extensively in the Philippines is to break a job into smaller parts and assign separate tasks to several Filipino contractors so that all of his eggs are not in one basket. This practice may entail a bit more work, but it is less risky.

How the Government Is Involved in Foreign Investment

Based in part on its long history as a colony, the Philippine government has enacted a number of laws regulating what types and levels of foreign investment it will allow. The Philippine government is not opposed to foreign investment, but its policies are not as wide open as a place like Hong Kong, where basically anything goes.

If you as a foreign investor desire to simply set up a company in the Philippines to do exporting (which is defined as exporting more than 60 percent of what you produce), then you can operate a wholly owned entity there. However, if your operations in the Philippines target the domestic economy, you will encounter certain limitations regarding where and whether you can invest and what percentage of ownership is permissible. In addition, some investments, such as those in mass media outlets, are completely out of bounds to outsiders as governed by the Foreign Investments Act of 1991 (FIA). This topic is obviously much too complex to discuss in detail in this chapter, so I recommend that foreign entities work closely with knowledgeable legal counsel in the Philippines during the planning stages of any foreign investment. Do not commit too many resources to setting up a company in the Philippines until you are certain it will be approved.

Ownership of real estate in the Philippines is also carefully controlled by the government, and as a general rule, foreign investors are not permitted to purchase land. One structure a foreign investor may consider is to form a joint venture with a Philippine partner in which the foreign company and the Philippine partner own 40 percent and 60 percent, respectively, of the acquired entity. The joint venture then leases the real estate back to the foreign investment vehicle. Again, this is an area that requires careful planning with Philippine legal counsel in order to avoid costly missteps.

Seven Points to Keep in Mind When Negotiating in the Philippines

Like everywhere in Asia, you must be culturally sensitive when negotiating in the Philippines and adapt your approaches to dealing with potential partners and customers. While there are no hard-and-fast rules, there are seven points about the Filipinos to always keep in mind.

Point One: Filipinos are Nonconfrontational

Filipinos generally do not enjoy direct confrontation; conflict makes them uncomfortable. While a negotiation with Koreans can quickly become confrontational, this rarely happens in the Philippines. Avoid confrontational language or pressure when dealing with the Filipinos. In fact, Filipinos love praise, and the more public the better; so you should find reasons to give them a pat on the back. This positive reinforcement will foster pride in your Filipino partners and also increase their loyalty and dedication to the job.

Point Two: Filipinos are Emotional

One reason I like the Filipinos is that they prefer to have business dealings with people as part of a whole relationship. Eye-to-eye contact is the best way to communicate with the Filipinos both socially and in business. Look them carefully in the eyes and explain your thoughts, asking for their understanding and input. When they respond with questions or replies that are not necessarily on point, it does not mean they are not listening; they are simply feeling their way around to better understand what you are suggesting. It is interesting how different the Filipino approach is from the style in Japan, where directly staring into someone's eyes is viewed as impolite.

Point Three: Never Put Filipinos in a Corner

Far too many American negotiators are strident in outlining "deal points" during the course of a negotiation and using this tactic to force an outcome. Do not try this technique in the Philippines. If you do, you will get one of two reactions. The first is what will appear to be a general agreement with what you are saying, but in fact it is not an agreement at all. The Filipinos are simply too polite to explain that what you are trying to force on them is unacceptable. The second possible reaction is that the Filipinos will essentially clam up and become nonresponsive. Unless they agree to what you propose, putting the Filipinos in a corner will be the end of your negotiation.

Point Four: Intuition

Because Filipinos by nature tend to be emotional, I have found them to be incredibly intuitive. They will recognize points that you are making without being told directly and will understand where you are going with a point before you have actually made it. There is no need to beat them over the head with your arguments. For some reason, there is an arrogant misconception among many Westerners that Filipinos are not good businesspeople, which is absolutely not true. Philippine businesspeople are world class in areas of education and ability. It is a mistake to underestimate them.

Point Five: Timing of Negotiations

Like elsewhere in Asia, never try to push through a negotiation in the Philippines too quickly. It is always a mistake to go into a negotiation saying you only have so many days or so many hours in which to complete a deal. Any schedule set in advance to govern a negotiation in the Philippines is bound to fail.

Point Six: The Collaborative Approach

In my experience, the best approach with the Filipinos is to begin discussions with general concepts and ideas and explain how both parties have similar needs, desires, and goals. The Filipinos will be more responsive to this gentle kind of approach, in which you seek to find a way to resolve any potential conflicts as collaborators and friends. Follow the natural rhythm of the negotiations. Once the parties agree to the general concepts and ideas, they can then begin drilling down to the details and contract specifics. Just be sure not to start with the specifics.

Point Seven: The Importance of Relationships

The more you can nurture a personal relationship with the Filipinos away from the negotiating table, the more successful you will be when discussions resume. Beneficial interactions include dinners, lunches, golf, or times just set aside for relaxation. If you find yourself invited to a Filipino home for dinner, definitely accept. You will have a good time, a great meal, and will know your hosts much better by the end of the evening.

Lawyers in the Philippines

There are many world-class law firms in the Philippines with as many or more lawyers educated in Western universities and law schools than probably anywhere else in Asia. While Filipino lawyers may not initially appear to be aggressive in a Western sense, do not be fooled. I have met many Filipino lawyers who are highly skilled and thoroughly understand Western needs and interests. When evaluating local counsel in the Philippines, I suggest you interview several firms. A law firm that is not only a dependable legal advisor but also has political ties will be beneficial in the Philippines. Such a firm will help you better navigate the challenges you may encounter when doing business in this interesting nation.

CHAPTER EIGHT

AMAZING SINGAPORE

If there is one universal rule in Asia, it is this: Never eat food from a street vendor. *But as with all rules, there is an exception—Singapore. Street vendors in Singapore are well known for hawking an infinite variety of foods representing all aspects of Asian cuisine. Customers can sample pretty much anything from grilled mud crabs to stewed shark head with soy and ginger, from fish maw and coconut curry noodle soups to garlic and chili omelets, and desserts of fried carrot cakes or shaved ice with sweet red bean paste. Foreigners can fully enjoy these delicacies without fear of becoming ill because Singapore licenses and strictly inspects all of its street vendors. Like absolutely everything else in Singapore, nothing is left to chance.*

From 1819 until the outbreak of World War II, the British controlled what is today's Singapore. The Japanese subsequently occupied Singapore until September 1945. During the following fourteen years of British rule, Singapore was increasingly allowed to engage in limited self-rule, which culminated in 1959 when Lee Kuan Yew became Singapore's prime minister. Lee Kuan Yew is universally venerated as the "George Washington of Singapore" to this day. Following its withdrawal from the British Commonwealth in 1963, Singapore merged into what was then known as the Federation of Malaysia. After two years of tumultuous conflict with the Malaysians, Singapore again desired to become independent, and finally elected to declare its sovereignty on August 9, 1965.

Like many of its Asian counterparts, Singapore was initially a very poor country. But, unlike its neighbors, tiny Singapore underwent one of the most amazing transformations of any country in the 20th century and morphed itself into one of the richest countries in the world.

No Corruption, Please!

Several global nonaligned nongovernmental organizations (NGOs), such as Transparency International, rank countries around the world as to transparency and level of (or lack of) institutional corruption. Every year Singapore finds itself at or near the top of the lists prepared by these independent organizations, while most of the other countries in Asia rank much lower. Singapore's high ranking is no fluke—the Singaporean government takes corruption extremely seriously.

When doing business in Singapore, you will probably never encounter direct or indirect suggestions from government officials to make more than just a good bid to win business. In my experience, the threat of or even appearance of corruption will not arise when negotiating in Singapore, particularly if you are dealing directly with government representatives. (Likewise, if you should be the one to suggest a bribe or "favor," expect to be banned and maybe even jailed.) This lack of institutional corruption makes doing business in Singapore easy for American companies, which must comply with the U.S. Foreign Corrupt Practices Act (FCPA) and its regulations.[1]

Negotiating with the Singaporeans

The welcome absence of institutional and governmental corruption in Singapore does not suggest, however, that negotiating with the Singaporeans is easy. The Singaporeans are hardheaded negotiators who are highly skilled at assembling complex contracts and transactions. They are also extremely competent, aggressive, and well prepared and will battle for every possible advantage.

Based on my personal experiences, including assisting a multinational company that sold a large infrastructure project to the

1. Now the British have passed their own toughly worded anticorruption statute, much like the FCPA.

Singapore government, I can attest to the Singaporeans' single-mindedness and exacting nature during negotiations. You should never assume that Singaporeans will later agree to change something on a "reasonable basis" if the obligation was not part of the parties' original contract. The lesson is to be as prepared and detailed as possible when negotiating with the Singaporeans—not just in the language of the contract but also in all points contained in the accompanying documentation.

Because of the transparency demanded by government officials, you will find that negotiations in Singapore are excruciatingly long and demanding. In addition, foreign corporations must compete for business against other highly competent global companies. The Singaporean procurement process itself is painstakingly slow because of the multiple levels of approval that are mandated in order to ensure the end result complies with Singaporean law. One advantage of doing business in Singapore is that funding a project is rarely an issue because Singapore is one of the richest countries in the world. If the Singaporean government really wants something, it has the funds to pay for it.

What about outside legal counsel? A foreign company negotiating business opportunities in Singapore is not required to enlist Singaporean legal counsel for assistance. Nevertheless, I recommend that any in-house counsel retain and work with local Singaporean lawyers throughout the process because there are unique aspects of Singaporean law which you need to be aware of, and experienced legal counsel can help you better understand the nuances of doing business in their country.

Once a contract is signed in Singapore, there is no "comeback," meaning if a term or requirement is clearly spelled out in the contract, then the Singaporeans will follow it to the letter and will be unlikely to amend it later if difficulties arise. A final written contract and its terms are respected in Singapore, unlike elsewhere in Asia (such as India or China) where contracts are constantly revised and massaged after execution in order to respond to new developments.

Hypothetically, assume your client has successfully signed a contract with the Singaporean government to supply a piece of equipment to be installed in a government power plant. It is common for commercial contracts in Singapore to provide for retention payments at the end of a project in the amount of 5 to 10 percent. The funds are retained by the government until the equipment has been fully tested and approved. The Singaporeans are very, very tough in exacting compliance with contract specifications. Even if the equipment is only slightly deficient in terms of the performance specs, do not expect the release of your retention monies until the specs are fully satisfied. The Singaporean courts will also uphold this strict construction of contracts. While Singapore is now independent, you will find that its views of contract drafting and interpretation were strongly influenced during its 100-plus years of colonization by the British. In conclusion, Singaporeans are sticklers for contractual performance, and no emotion or sentiment will be present during or after negotiations are complete.

The Role of the Singaporean Government

Singapore's government prides itself on being exceptionally receptive to outside investment. Unlike other countries in Southeast Asia that take a more conservative view, foreign investors are typically free to conduct business in Singapore without the need for a local partner. Moreover, Singaporeans are far from leery of outside investors and court them openly.

There are a variety of ways to conduct business in Singapore, but the most common strategy is to form a limited liability company. Other formation options include using a branch of a foreign corporation as a general partnership, a kind of limited liability partnership, or a sole proprietorship. While foreign investment in Singapore is encouraged, every business in the country, whether it involves a foreign investor or not, must register with the Singapore Accounting and Corporate Regulatory Authority (known as ACRA). The underlying philosophy of ACRA is that all businesses must identify individuals who will take on legal responsibility for the firm's activities. For a Singaporean company, you must designate at least one director; if you are doing business as a branch of a foreign corporation, two agents are required. One of the nominated individuals must be Singaporean, a permanent resident of Singapore, or a person who has permission from the Singaporean government to legally work in Singapore. The concept is to have a "responsible person" that the Singaporean government can readily identify to take responsibility for compliance with all local rules and regulations.

One word of caution for foreigners—be wary of becoming a director of a Singaporean company because it comes with serious legal responsibilities. If the Singaporean company encounters problems, serving as a director will carry with it both personal and legal liabilities. For example, if a worker on a construction project is killed in Singapore and it is determined that there were safety violations for which the Singaporean company might be responsible, then the individual directors (whether Singaporean or not) can be held accountable both civilly and possibly criminally. In such a case, the foreign director could have his or her passport held by the Singaporean government pending an investigation into the incident. The best advice is to carefully review Singaporean law as to the liabilities of outside directors before naming one of your company's key executives as a director of a Singaporean venture.

Local Agents and Distributors in Singapore

Unlike elsewhere in Asia, the rules governing the relationship and obligations between a foreign company and a local agent or distributor in Singapore are largely a matter of contract. If an issue arises, Singaporean courts will generally follow the provisions of the contract agreed to by the parties, unless the provisions are commercially unreasonable or in conflict with Singaporean laws.

It is important to note that Singapore does have several statutes on its books that provide protection for consumers against sellers (in this case, agents or representatives) who engage in unfair practices. For example, the Sale of Goods Act (Chapter 393) addresses how goods may be sold within Singapore and places specific obligations on sellers (agents and/or distributors) as to the quality and how the goods are described. Another example is Singapore's Multi-Level Marketing and Pyramid Selling (Prohibition) Act, which prohibits companies from engaging in pyramid schemes in both the sale of goods and services. Of course, legitimate insurance businesses and master franchises are permitted in Singapore, but a foreign company should closely examine Singaporean laws before authorizing an agent or distributor to conduct sales in the company's name.

MERGERS AND ACQUISITIONS IN SINGAPORE

In most cases, mergers and acquisitions involving foreign investors are liberally permitted by the Singaporean government, which seeks to attract qualified foreign investors. However, certain sectors of the economy are strictly regulated, including the ownership of airlines, power companies, and port facilities. In addition, while Singapore is a democracy, its government maintains strict laws controlling content published in the print and electronic media. The Singaporean government will specifically restrict the publication of materials that it considers to be politically sensitive. Offshore magazines and newspapers cannot be sold in Singapore unless a permit is granted by the government in advance, and Singaporean government officials are extremely sensitive to foreign publications that appear to interfere with or comment unfavorably on domestic politics in Singapore. There have been cases in Singapore in the past where foreign publications such as *The Economist* have come into direct conflict with Singaporean authorities and were subsequently sued for libel. Similar restrictions exist in Singapore regarding public broadcasting and media.

Interestingly, the Singaporean government is quite liberal when it comes to regulations over the ownership of telecommunications services. Since April 2000, any company wishing to be involved in telecommunications in Singapore can invest without limits on the amount of equity—in stark contrast to the restrictions imposed by other Asian countries.

Employment Regulations in Singapore

Singapore has a population of approximately 5 million people, including nonresidents. While the country's indigenous population is largely Chinese, there is also a large Indian minority as well as representatives of almost every other ethnic group throughout Asia. Singapore is unique because more than one-third of its population is composed of foreigners, and the country's basic employment laws apply to both Singaporeans and outsiders.

Singapore's primary law regulating employment is the Employment Act, the key focus of which is protecting those employees in Singapore who earn less than about $1,200 USD per month. The Employment Act, which specifically outlines what holidays, sick leave, and other minimum benefits workers are entitled to receive from their employers, is very effective at protecting those workers who earn salaries at the lower end of the pay scale. It is important to remember that the provisions of this act take precedence over any contract an employee signs if the contract tries to limit the rights conferred on employees pursuant to the act. Not surprisingly, most foreign workers who hold executive or managerial positions are exempt from the provisions of the act because of the salary thresholds, so their benefits are determined solely by the contract they sign with their employer in Singapore.

Intellectual Property Laws in Singapore

A discussion of intellectual property law in Singapore may be refreshingly brief. Singapore has signed twelve major international conventions for the protection of intellectual property and actively participates in international enforcement activities. It is fair to say that Singapore places a higher priority on enforcing intellectual property rights (both foreign and domestic) than any other country in Asia (except perhaps Japan). In fact, the Singaporean police have established a specialized division of knowledgeable officers whose only job it is to investigate intellectual property rights violations. In addition, the court system in Singapore seats judges who are not only knowledgeable about intellectual property issues but also willing to take aggressive steps to enforce the rights of intellectual property owners, whether or not they are Singaporean. Singapore's staunch support of intellectual property rights is a key reason the country has long been a favored locale for regional headquarters of multinational corporations doing business in Asia. Any foreign businessperson can take comfort in knowing that intellectual property protection is alive and well in Singapore.

DISPUTE RESOLUTION IN SINGAPORE

When drafting a commercial contract in Singapore, the parties need to decide whether to provide for adjudication by local courts or to specify arbitration if a dispute arises. The court system in Singapore is independent and staffed with judges who are well trained and rarely influenced by outside forces, which is not always the case elsewhere in Asia. The independence of the country's judiciary is guaranteed by the Constitution of Singapore. The structure and administration of Singapore's court system provides further evidence of the legacy of British colonization. Consequently, foreign companies need not be concerned about political pressures in Singapore when having a commercial case resolved there.

The alternative to using Singapore's courts for dispute resolution is to elect international arbitration. Singapore prides itself on being a genuine center for international arbitration. Moreover, because of Singapore's desire to attract and retain the headquarters of foreign multinational corporations, the country has devoted a great deal of attention and resources to promoting Singapore as a good place to arbitrate disputes.

From the legislative perspective, Singapore has enacted both an International Arbitration Act and a separate Arbitration Act. If a contract does not specifically address the details of how an arbitration is to be conducted in Singapore, one of these acts will outline the applicable arbitration procedures. Not surprisingly, Singapore is also a strong advocate and adoptee of the New York Convention on the Recognition and Enforcement of Foreign Arbitral Awards.

To institutionalize arbitration, Singapore has supported a major semiprivate and well-recognized arbitral body called the Singapore International Arbitration Centre (SIAC). SIAC maintains a highly qualified and diverse panel of potential arbitrators who may be selected to resolve disputes. Based on my experiences, you can be comfortable with naming SIAC as a reliable arbitration tribunal in your international contacts.

CHAPTER NINE

THE OTHER CHINAS: HONG KONG AND TAIWAN

The best and least expensive way to experience firsthand the hustle and bustle of today's Hong Kong costs about 30 cents and takes only ten minutes. For more than 100 years, the Star Ferry has continuously shuttled commuters and tourists back and forth between Hong Kong's central business district and the pier at Tsim Sha Sui in Kowloon. From the double-deck ferries, the changes in and dynamics of Hong Kong are evident everywhere you look. Everyone—from the passengers to those hawking business suits and knockoff watches outside the ferry entrance—has something to do and is in a hurry to do it. Some feared that Hong Kong would waste away after its turnover from the British in 1997. The skeptics were wrong.

While Chapter Five focuses on the People's Republic of China (PRC), there are two "other Chinas," Hong Kong SAR and Taiwan ROC, neither of which should be overlooked. Both are as different from the PRC as they are from each other, so an understanding of how to conduct business in the PRC is of little help when it comes to Hong Kong and Taiwan.

Hong Kong SAR: The World of Hong Kong

More than 160 years ago, Hong Kong was a sleepy fishing village perched precariously on the southern coast of China. By the early 19th century, throughout the region bitter conflicts over trade goods and opium were occurring between the Chinese and the English. The British ultimately gained the upper hand and colonized the then nondescript village of Hong Kong. Through the years, Hong Kong grew and eventually emerged as one of the world's major financial centers, despite its small physical size and its 7 million closely packed residents. Hong Kong's stock market, known as the Hang Seng, is now an increasingly active player in issuing global equities. Today, Hong Kong is one of the foremost regions for global trade, and for some outsiders remains the gateway to the PRC.

Many experts predicted that significant changes would occur when England's "lease" on Hong Kong expired in 1997, at which time the rights to control Hong Kong reverted to the central government of the PRC. Hong Kong was renamed Hong Kong SAR; SAR stands for Special Administrative Region and signifies that Hong Kong is now part of the PRC. During years of protracted negotiations leading up to the turnover in June 1997, the English and the Chinese hammered out a special deal under which Hong Kong would be granted the right to govern itself semiautonomously for fifty years after its return to the PRC's control. The parties' underlying intent was to allow people living in Hong Kong to remain partially, though not fully, independent of the level of governmental oversight that exists throughout the PRC.

As opposed to the PRC, Hong Kong maintains a judiciary that is relatively independent and oversees a legal system based on a common law approach. While Hong Kong retains a multiparty political system, some limitations are imposed by the PRC on what powers the Hong Kong legislative body can and cannot exercise. After some initial skirmishes on policy issues, it appears that Hong Kong and the PRC have reached an accommodation giving each party what it wants—at least for now.

Establishing a Company in Hong Kong

The economy of Hong Kong is as wide open and unrestricted as any throughout Asia. For decades, this hands-off approach has enticed entrepreneurs to establish and conduct businesses in Hong Kong, even when many of them were really targeting opportunities on the PRC's mainland. Hong Kong was a comfortable outpost.

The government does, however, impose certain restrictions on doing business in Hong Kong. First, foreign investors need to be aware of Hong Kong's new money laundering regulations, which require compliance with the global clampdown on money coming from and going to questionable sources. When establishing a company in Hong Kong, the principals are now required to identify all of the individuals who are responsible for setting up the company and managing its operations once formed. This regulatory oversight is not onerous, but may become increasingly strict in the future. The government has also enacted anticorruption laws, which are strictly enforced by local Hong Kong authorities. The penalties for engaging in corrupt activities are severe and frequently imposed.

The procedure for establishing a limited liability company in Hong Kong is relatively fast and simple once it has been confirmed that the desired corporate name (English and/or Chinese) is available. The remainder of the incorporation process can be accomplished in less than ten days, assuming all required documentation and backup information are readily available. If faced with the need to set up a Hong Kong entity very quickly, most law firms in Hong Kong can provide their clients with a "shell company" that can be prepared in as few as three to five business days.

Hong Kong law is quite liberal regarding the formation of limited liability companies. Either an individual or a foreign (non-Chinese) company can incorporate a limited liability company in Hong Kong, and the incorporator can act without facing the kind of bureaucratic challenges typically imposed in China. A Hong Kong limited liability company is not required to have a local representative involved in the incorporation process, and the costs of establishing a Hong Kong limited liability company are not excessive. Foreign investors can expect to pay approximately $12,000 HK to a Hong Kong law firm to incorporate a simple entity, in addition to required disbursements totaling about $3,000 HK. These standard costs will increase for companies requiring a more complex structure or in need of specialized legal advice.

Hong Kong law does require each domestic limited liability company to maintain a physical location for conducting business. Consequently, foreign investors must either lease office space in Hong Kong or acquire an actual location where the tax authorities and other parties can find the company. It is not uncommon for a director of a Hong Kong limited liability company in Hong Kong to use his or her residential address for the business. I caution against this practice, however, because once a residence has been established as the official business address, then any papers or documents sent to that address are presumptively received by the limited liability company. In addition, if the director is ever fired, the company may not receive official correspondence sent by the government or other bureaus and agencies. Finally, many residences located in Hong Kong are prohibited from operating a business on what is zoned as a residential property.

My recommendation when setting up a Hong Kong entity is to elect to have the company's initial address sited at the Hong Kong lawyer's office. Most law firms will charge only a minimal fee (approximately $5,000 HK per year) to maintain a company's registered office address, which is inexpensive insurance against future problems. The address can always be changed once the Hong Kong company becomes established in a permanent location. The advantage of using a law firm is that foreign investors can rest assured that all filings will be made on behalf of the company, and its principals will be kept advised of any formal documentation that arrives at the registered office.

The Language of Business in Hong Kong

About 95 percent of the 7 million people living in Hong Kong are of Chinese origin. Most of Hong Kong's residents at one time left the mainland and relocated to Hong Kong for political and/or economic reasons. It is important to note that there are two official languages in Hong Kong—Chinese and English. However, the spoken Chinese language most often used is Cantonese, not Mandarin. You will discover that those fluent in Mandarin probably do not understand Cantonese, and vice versa. Mandarin is spoken in most of the PRC, except in the South where Cantonese predominates.

The English language was extremely prevalent throughout Hong Kong until the turnover in 1997 because the United Kingdom's colonial government made it a point to educate children

(Chinese and expatriates, or expats) at most grade levels in English. After the turnover, there was a period in which the English language was deemphasized and Chinese—in most cases, Cantonese—was substituted. In my view, this language substitution adversely affected the multinational companies and their expat employees living and doing business in Hong Kong because they relied heavily on English. In recent years, it has become clear that the Hong Kong government is once again emphasizing the importance of English. That being said, it is not uncommon to get into a taxicab in Hong Kong and discover that the driver speaks no English and may not even recognize the name of your well-known hotel. Consequently, it pays to carry a card with you at all times in Hong Kong bearing the name of your hotel in both English and Chinese and to have a Chinese colleague write for you in Chinese the address of your destination. This simple practice will help foreign travelers avoid problems. For the more adventurous who can forgo a taxi, I highly recommend the Hong Kong public transportation systems, which are excellent and have signs posted everywhere in both English and Chinese.

Hong Kong as a Base for Asian Operations

For decades, Hong Kong has maintained a strong reputation as a regional administrative destination for multinational corporations wishing to do business in China as well as elsewhere throughout Asia. Singapore also works hard to attract global corporate headquarters and remains Hong Kong's major competitor. Both countries are good choices for foreign companies seeking to establish an Asian base of operations.

After 1997, many observers predicted that the number of regional headquarters of multinational corporations located in Hong Kong would rapidly diminish. Although some losses occurred, Hong Kong remains an attractive destination for multinational corporations that require an Asian regional headquarters but do not specifically need to be located in China. One advantage of choosing Hong Kong over another Chinese mainland location such as Shanghai is the widespread use of the English language in Hong Kong. Also,

Hong Kong is a safe place to live for both Chinese and foreigners and has a wonderful public transportation system. With an "Octopus Card," you can go just about anywhere in Hong Kong and even up to Shenzhen or Guangzhou via train. One particular advantage of Hong Kong for foreigners is that there are a number of high-quality international schools for children of expats living there.

One downside of Hong Kong is its environment and poor air quality. It is worth noting though that Hong Kong itself is not necessarily to blame for its environmental problems. Hong Kong lies downwind from tens of thousands of factories located in the Pearl River Delta, where much of the world's manufacturing capacity resides. The factory output in the Pearl River Delta makes it the 16th-largest economy in the world. Because of the direction of the winds, much of the polluted air generated by the factories ends up blowing over Hong Kong and Kowloon. The Hong Kong government is attempting to combat this environmental challenge, but it will remain an issue for many years to come. Nevertheless, the air quality and environmental problems in most Chinese cities are much worse than those present in Hong Kong.

Intellectual Property in Hong Kong

Before the 1997 turnover, intellectual property was always a high priority for the Hong Kong government because of the city's status as a major global trade center. Most of the multinational corporations doing business in Hong Kong also considered patents, trademarks, and copyrights essential to the success of their business models.

Following the turnover, there has been very little change, if any, in how intellectual property is protected within Hong Kong. Unlike judges in other parts of Asia, Hong Kong's judiciary generally understands intellectual property rights and boasts a strong record of enforcement against infringement. The people and courts of Hong Kong are too smart to kill the goose that lays the golden egg!

Courts versus Arbitration

The judiciary in Hong Kong has a far better reputation for quality and fairness than most other countries in Asia. Little or no political influence is exerted over the judicial system on purely commercial matters before the courts, and this has been fairly consistent over the last three or four decades. Nevertheless, I recommend that foreign companies select dispute resolution by means of arbitration as opposed to the local court systems in most commercial situations in Hong Kong.

Multinational corporations that choose arbitration to resolve commercial disputes frequently utilize two major independent arbitral tribunals located in Asia, one of which is in Hong Kong and the other of which is in Singapore. The Hong Kong International Arbitration Centre (HKIAC) has an excellent and well-deserved reputation for resolving commercial disputes between Chinese and non-Chinese parties in an impartial manner. The HKIAC website (www.hkiac.org) is quite helpful for interested parties. The HKIAC was formed in the mid-1980s as foreign investment targeted at China boomed, and investors inevitably ran into problems. The HKIAC maintains a list of qualified arbitrators, many of whom are fluent in both Chinese and English. Conveniently located in Hong Kong's central business district, the HKIAC offices even have rooms that can be rented for a reasonable fee to accommodate arbitrations. I recommend you strongly consider selecting the HKIAC as the forum in which to resolve disputes in international contracts involving the Chinese. While China has its own form of arbitration (CIETAC, which is discussed elsewhere in this book), the HKIAC has many positive aspects.

American and European companies (or their legal counsel) that insist upon having their commercial arbitrations with Chinese entities conducted in New York, London, or Paris often encounter significant, unexpected hurdles. Even assuming that jurisdiction is appropriate in those venues (which is questionable), logistical problems are posed when Chinese witnesses require visas and permission to travel outside of China to attend or testify at the arbitration.

Because the HKIAC has established a working relationship with arbitral tribunals in China, it is much easier for Chinese nationals living on the mainland to travel to Hong Kong to participate in arbitration than it is to travel elsewhere.

While there is no hard-and-fast rule, it has been my experience that final arbitral decisions properly rendered by the HKIAC stand a better chance of being enforced by Chinese courts on the mainland as opposed to the awards of other arbitral tribunals that are decided outside of China or Hong Kong.

Lawyers and Law Firms in Hong Kong

Hong Kong is filled with lawyers of all types, nationalities, and skill levels. Aside from the very small law firms that exist solely to represent local residents with small commercial problems, there are two major types of law firms that a foreign investor should consider retaining for legal advice on doing business in China and Hong Kong.

The first type is sometimes referred to in slang as an Anglo firm and is often a branch office of a major international law firm. Many of these firms, particularly those that are headquartered in the United Kingdom or the United States, are heavily staffed with lawyers who are not Chinese (though some are likely to have lived in Hong Kong for years). Some pundits who dislike these firms refer to their lawyers in private as FILTH (i.e., Failed in London, Tried Hong Kong), a characterization that is totally unfair. These firms are generally high quality with price structures to match. Without question the prices charged by top lawyers in Hong Kong rival those in London or New York. The downside is that there are fewer well-placed Chinese lawyers who were born in Hong Kong and understand the marketplace working there than elsewhere.

The second alternative is to seek out a strictly Chinese law firm in Hong Kong, meaning a law firm which is comprised of lawyers who are ethnically Chinese. These firms can vary in size, but their top two or three partners are inevitably highly experienced in doing business in China and run their firms with a strong hand. Most lawyers in Hong Kong–based Chinese law firms fluently speak both English and Chinese because they have been trained in schools around the world. Surprisingly, many of these lawyers received their legal or university training in the West. Lawyers in Chinese-dominated firms often have extensive experience in negotiating with businesspeople both in Hong Kong and on the mainland because of family and historical ties.

Since both types of firms have advantages and disadvantages, I suggest foreign companies interview a few of each before making a final decision on local counsel.

Taiwan ROC: The Enigma of Taiwan

Japan gave up any claims to the islands that comprise what is today's Taiwan following its defeat in World War II. Later, as tensions on China's mainland came to a head between the followers of Chang Kai-shek and Mao Tse-tung during the late 1940s, Chang Kai-shek relocated himself and hundreds of thousands of his followers to Taiwan, where they set up a government known as the Republic of China (ROC).

For a period during the 1950s, Taiwan, particularly the islands of Quemoy and Matsu, almost led China and the United States to the brink of war. These two islands lie less than a dozen miles off the coast of the People's Republic of China and were claimed by both Taiwan and China. At the time, no one knew whether the United States would come to the defense of Formosa (today's Republic of China) if the Chinese invaded Quemoy and Matsu. The Chinese were furious with the policy of the American government and threatened retaliation. During the time of the famous televised debates between Senator John F. Kennedy and then Vice President Richard M. Nixon in 1960, Candidate Nixon warned of the dangers posed by China to Taiwan and the rest of the world. A decade later, Nixon, then president, reversed the old policy by advocating direct relations with China: "The Chinese are a great and vital people who should not remain isolated from the international community. . . . It is certainly in our interest, and in the interest of peace and stability in Asia and the world, that we take what steps we can toward improved political relations with Peking" (Richard M. Nixon, *First Foreign Policy Report to Congress*, February 1970). Nixon's actions defused the tensions among China, the United States, and Taiwan.

Since the 1970s, political tensions between the Republic of China and the People's Republic of China have continued, but at a far less heightened level. In my view, it is highly unlikely that the People's Republic of China will go to war to contest ownership of Taiwan. Although there are nationalists living in Taiwan who still believe that Taiwan should openly declare itself an independent country and be free of any territorial claims of the PRC, most observers believe that a merger of interests between Taiwan and the People's Republic of China is only a matter of time.

Inbound Investment in Taiwan

While Hong Kong is wide open to all foreign investors with very few limitations on what they can do, doing business in Taiwan is more difficult. Taiwan imposes a detailed approval process over any direct investment contemplated by an outside investor. The primary areas of concern for Taiwanese officials are foreign investors and investors (foreign or Taiwanese) who conduct business in certain industries that the government considers subject to its control. Foreign Investment Approval (FIA) must be issued by the Investment Commission of the Ministry of Economic Affairs (MOEA). For smaller investments, approval is granted relatively quickly (usually within a week). For larger investments, particularly in financial institutions, telecommunications companies, and real estate, MOEA will make a much more detailed examination and take a longer time to decide. The point is the Taiwanese are usually willing to allow foreign investors to conduct business in Taiwan without a local partner, as long as the investment targets certain industrial sectors favored by the government. Foreign ownership is severely curtailed in other industries such as shipping, railway transportation, the media, utilities, and general aviation.

In short, my guidance is to consult with Taiwanese lawyers who can provide good, practical guidance early in the investment process. The lawyers with the better firms in Taiwan are well trained and comfortable with answering questions and addressing the requirements of multinational corporations.

Intellectual Property Laws in Taiwan

Thirty years ago, Taiwan was considered one of the worst places in the world to do business if you were the owner of a valuable technology or intellectual property. Almost everything IP-based in Taiwan was at risk of being stolen. Even worse, the courts did little or nothing to defend the rights of intellectual property owners who were foreigners or even Taiwanese. Taiwan's attitude toward intellectual property protection has shifted significantly in the last thirty years. Taiwan now boasts a good reputation for protecting intellectual property owned either by Taiwanese nationals or foreigners. The reason for this change in attitude is not philosophical, but rather economic.

In the 1980s, for every ten Taiwanese university students studying engineering or the sciences in the United States and elsewhere, only two came back. Very few Taiwanese companies were offering good career opportunities for those new engineers and scientists, which created a damaging "brain drain" for Taiwan. As the promise of intellectual property protection increased during the 1990s, more foreign-educated engineers returned home, and as a result Taiwan now is the headquarters for many leading manufacturing and technology companies. In my opinion, foreign companies can expect that their intellectual property will be easier to protect in Taiwan than in most other places throughout Asia.

Dispute Resolution

Taiwan is not a signatory to the New York Convention on the Recognition and Enforcement of Foreign Arbitral Awards. The New York Convention is why international arbitration is so widely used throughout Asia. For this reason, as a foreign investor in Taiwan or as a Taiwanese company, you are likely to want to resolve your commercial disputes in Taiwanese courts as opposed to using international arbitration. This is the exact opposite of what I recommend for Hong Kong and for many other countries throughout Asia. Because Taiwan is not a signatory, you would encounter significant problems in trying to transfer an arbitration decision that was rendered outside of Taiwan and have it enforced in Taiwan.

Doing Business in Taiwan and China

There was a time when your company could encounter problems if you had manufacturing or other activities located in Taiwan and then tried to do business in the PRC. In short, those days are past. On a commercial level, relations between Taiwan and the PRC have never been closer. The only thing that could upset this is if China and Taiwan came to a political impasse that escalated out of control. However, I think the probability of that happening is extremely remote. In June 2010, Chinese and Taiwanese negotiators signed what is likely to become a landmark agreement. The Economic Cooperation Framework Agreement (ECFA) should further cement close economic exchanges in the coming years.

CHAPTER TEN

INDONESIA ON THE RISE

From the beginning of time, every culture has developed its own inimitable ways of passing along stories from one generation to the next. Indonesia provides one of the most unique examples of traditional storytelling with its "wayang tales," which are based on epics that originated in India but made their way to Java (part of today's Indonesia) more than a thousand years ago. Most wayang tales are classic good versus evil stories brought to life by Wayang Kulit—handmade shadow puppets constructed of leather or paper that is intricately cut, meticulously shaped, and brightly painted. This ancient form of puppet theater, often accompanied by music and dancing, draws enormous audiences with performances lasting well into the night.

Even though Indonesia ranks as the fourth-largest country in the world by population, with more than 240 million inhabitants, it remains one of the least understood Asian countries. Indonesia is not usually on the radar screen of multinational companies unless they are dealing in energy, natural resources, or agricultural products. Overlooking Indonesia is a mistake, however, because it promises to emerge as a real economic powerhouse on the world stage over the next few decades.

The Dutch colonized what is today's Indonesia in the early 17th century. The famous East India Company helped to spearhead the effort, which enabled the Dutch to extract billions of dollars in natural resources and commodities from its prosperous colony for more than 300 years. The Dutch were attracted to the islands of Indonesia because they were located on a key sea trade route in the geographic center of Asia. Most of the ships sailing between East and West passed directly through Indonesian waters, so it was a natural place for the Dutch to locate their trading activities.

Originally those who lived in Indonesia practiced the Hindu and Buddhist religions almost exclusively. It was only in the 17th century that most Indonesians converted to the Muslim faith. Today, Indonesia is home to the largest concentration of Muslims anywhere in the world, registering 86 percent of its population. Despite the prevalence of practicing Muslims, Indonesia remains culturally diverse.

Indonesia finally gained its independence from the Dutch following the end of World War II. At the time, the new Indonesian government adopted a national constitution that guaranteed, among other entitlements, religious freedoms. Under Indonesia's constitution, five religions in addition to Islam are officially recognized, meaning that while Indonesia as a country has the largest Muslim population in the world, it is not a Muslim state.

The Twisted Path of Indonesian Independence

Nearly 350 years of Dutch colonization of Indonesia ended with the War in the Pacific. The Japanese invaded Indonesia in early 1942, and the Dutch withdrew in 1945. A national Indonesian leader named Sukarno appointed himself as the first president of the newly minted country of Indonesia and fought both the Dutch and the English for the next four years. In late 1949, the United States of Indonesia was officially recognized with Sukarno as its head. Under Sukarno, Indonesia suffered severe economic dislocations and bloody rivalries between ethnic groups, and several times during the 1950s the annual inflation rate exceeded 1,000 percent. Simply put, Indonesia under Sukarno's rule was an economic disaster with ongoing national political strife.

During the turbulent decade of the 1960s, another national figure by the name of Suharto rose to prominence. Then a lieutenant general in the Indonesian Army, Suharto came into direct conflict with Sukarno and his followers. Suharto eventually assumed power in Indonesia by creating a government that was openly controlled by the Indonesian military. Over the next thirty-two years, the government under Suharto was a reflection of extremes. By focusing on encouraging inbound foreign investment, Suharto was able to suppress the massive runaway inflation that plagued Indonesia during the 1950s. Eventually the depressed Indonesian economy was replaced with nearly thirty years of positive economic growth. This upward economic swing benefited nearly everyone in the country, though the rich, as it became obvious over time, received disproportionately more of the spoils. Without question, those individuals with close relationships with the Suharto family and government figures prospered the most. One downside of the Suharto regime was that it was difficult to do business in Indonesia without making "payments" to government officials. Those payments, allegedly extracted in order to approve investments, encouraged widespread corruption throughout Indonesian society.

The Suharto regime came to an end when the Asian financial crisis of 1997 hit Indonesia particularly hard. During one six-week period in 1997, the value of Indonesia's currency dropped by about 25 percent. Suharto finally resigned as president under heavy political pressure from opposition demonstrators. In a criminal investigation of Suharto following his resignation, it was revealed (to the surprise of few) that members of his family had improperly acquired billions of dollars in assets during the time he controlled Indonesia. Suharto's son was later sent to jail in 2002 on various corruption charges.

It is important for foreign companies trying to do business in Indonesia to understand the country's political history, especially the fifty-year period of intense institutional corruption that greatly influenced how government policy decisions were made in the past. Now, the current president of Indonesia, Susilo Bambang Yudhoyono, has taken a position of strong opposition to institutional corruption, and his efforts have been embraced by the public. Consequently, corruption in Indonesia is noticeably less prevalent today, but foreign companies still need to be extremely careful in any dealings with government officials or as partners in commercial joint ventures in which the government may have an interest.

Financial Transactions in Indonesia

There are four important financial issues to keep in mind when evaluating potential transactions in Indonesia.

Currency

Business transactions between a foreign company and an Indonesian party are typically conducted in U.S. dollars (USD) rather than the local Indonesian currency, the rupiah (IDR). The Indonesian government has been fairly liberal in allowing foreign currencies and the rupiah to be freely exchanged and transferred. Although the Bank of Indonesia requires the filing of a report describing each transfer of funds in excess of $10,000 USD sent outside Indonesia, most funds are repatriated without any problems or objections from local officials. The foregoing generalization, however, presumes that the repatriation of funds (U.S. dollars or otherwise) is a result of a transfer to settle a contractual obligation or a repatriation of profits or licensing fees to a foreign party.

Letters of Credit

For commercial payment obligations, banks in Indonesia commonly issue letters of credit. Indonesia's central bank has power over most such transactions within the country and has a favorable history of not interfering in commercial deals. Still, it is wise for foreign companies to confirm all letters of credit with their own banks at home whenever possible.

Taxation

Corporate taxation in Indonesia is fairly straightforward as compared to the taxation practices of its neighboring countries. Similar to the practice in the United States, taxes can be imposed on a company at both the provincial (state) level and by the central government in Indonesia. The two major taxes used to generate revenue for the government are the value-added tax (VAT) and the income tax. Indonesia also imposes a myriad of other minor taxes on companies that vary depending on the type of industry involved. Fortunately, Indonesia is a signatory to several tax treaties with countries around the world that serve to eliminate double taxation on profits coming out of Indonesia.

Capital Investment

The Capital Investment Coordinating Board is the Indonesian agency with the power to regulate which investments are permissible in Indonesia and which are not. In the past, Indonesia had a convoluted bureaucracy that was exceedingly difficult for foreign investors to navigate, but the current administration under President Yudhoyono is working to simplify the investment approval process. With certain statutory exceptions, a foreign company can do business in Indonesia without a local partner so long as it forms an Indonesian PMA (foreign investment company). One key factor Indonesian government officials examine during the PMA approval process is the entity's level of capitalization, which must be adequate to meet the needs of its proposed venture.

Dispute Resolution in Indonesia

When planning a venture in Indonesia, the issue of how to resolve commercial disputes needs to be addressed up-front. While most foreign investors tend to automatically elect to place arbitration provisions in their commercial contracts in other countries in Asia, the choice to forgo dispute resolution by courts is far less common in Indonesia, for several reasons. One reason for this tendency is the long history of commercial conflicts that have occurred between foreign multinational corporations that have conducted business in Indonesia and native Indonesians. Much of the strife stems comes from numerous instances of inappropriate exploitation of Indonesian resources by foreign multinationals. Another factor is a pattern of widespread corruption of public officials that has made Indonesians wary of foreign investments. Based on the foregoing, how and where to resolve such disputes is a key issue that should not be underestimated.

While Indonesia is a member of the New York Convention on the Recognition and Enforcement of Foreign Arbitral Awards, this membership alone is not definitive. In commercial contracts where arbitration is selected as the method to resolve disputes, the Singapore International Arbitration Centre (SIAC), which is discussed in greater detail in Chapter Eight, is geographically close to Indonesia and a good option to consider. A 90-minute flight from Jakarta allows a foreign company to arbitrate its dispute in Singapore where the English language is used and the results and decisions are made by a selected member of their panel.

Before automatically selecting arbitration over courts for dispute resolution in Indonesia, there is an important practical consideration: whether the Indonesian party involved in the transaction has any significant assets located outside of Indonesia. If it does, then it makes sense to name SIAC as the body for resolving disputes in your contracts, because an award issued by SIAC can be enforced against the assets of an Indonesian company held outside of Indonesia. Another option is utilizing the Hong Kong International Arbitration Centre (HKIAC). However, if the Indonesian company with which you may have a dispute has assets located only within Indonesia, then you need to rethink how to proceed. Historically, the Indonesian courts have been reluctant to enforce arbitration judgments issued outside Indonesia against an Indonesian company in Indonesia. In that case, you may be better off resorting to Indonesian courts in trying to resolve disputes or, more to the point, having arbitration decide the matter in Indonesia, where it is easier to enforce a favorable judgment entered on your behalf. I recommend you discuss these alternatives with Indonesian legal counsel before making your final decision.

Women in Business in Indonesia

Although nearly 90 percent of Indonesians are members of the Muslim faith, that fact does not necessarily influence the role of women in business in Indonesia. The Indonesian constitution guarantees women within its society the right to vote and hold the same rights of citizenship as men. Do not be surprised when you encounter women in Indonesia holding responsible positions in the provincial and national governments as well as corporations. Simply put, women are equal to men in the eyes of the law. Taking it a step further, if you are an American or European woman representing your client's or company's interests, you should have no reservations about traveling to Indonesia and conducting business there. As long as you show due respect and deference to the dominant religion in Indonesia, you will find yourself accepted as an equal in negotiations and business dealings. Because Indonesians tend to dress formally in most business circumstances, women (and men) should simply wear clothing that is conservative so as not to unintentionally insult those with whom they meet. In this way, Indonesia is a unique mixture of attitudes spanning the traditional versus modern approaches to business. The view of women in Indonesia, in my opinion, is unlikely to change much in the future.

Relationships and Negotiating in Indonesia

Most of Indonesia's population is indigenous. The two largest subgroups are the Javanese (who represent 42 percent of the total population) and the Sundanese. There is also a diverse array of other smaller ethnic groups in Indonesia, such as the Chinese (representing 8 percent of the population) and ethnic Malays (representing 7 percent of the population). There has been a long history of tension between the Chinese Indonesians and the non-Chinese Indonesians going back centuries. The reason is basically economic—while small in size, the Chinese business community has traditionally controlled a disproportionately large portion of the wealth within the Indonesian economy, leading to simmering resentments that sometimes turned violent.

Setting aside the ethnic Chinese, Indians, and Malays living in Indonesia, one can make certain generalizations about the majority of Indonesians. To begin, most Indonesians possess warm and outgoing personalities. As a general rule, Indonesians tend to be modest and nonconfrontational in their personal and business relationships. Unlike the Koreans, the Indonesians will rarely challenge you in a business negotiation. In fact, the opposite is true. If an Indonesian is uncomfortable dealing with a tough point during a negotiation, he or she will probably smile and say something like, "I understand your view" or "I appreciate the importance of this issue to your company." Pay close attention, and do not make the mistake of thinking you have concurrence from your Indonesian counterpart on the contentious point; you do not. In Indonesian culture, disagreement is not supposed to rise to the surface due in large part to the concept of *face*, which appears frequently throughout this book. Face means the Indonesians do not want to object to you because it may cause one of you (in their perception) to lose face. Even more important, if you push for an answer or a response in a public forum, your Indonesian counterpart is likely to either say nothing or appear to agree with you if it gets you to back off. Because of the checkered past of foreign multinationals in Indonesia and their reputation for being overbearing, foreign parties will have an even harder time reaching agreement with Indonesians during negotiations.

This book's Chapter Five, on China, describes how the Chinese view a contract as a whole document and not a set of individually negotiated points. The Chinese view is quite similar to how Indonesians view contracts. If your Indonesian counterpart is not satisfied with the contract as it appears once the negotiation is nearing an end, then expect him or her to back away, even if you have had general point-by-point agreement all along. That said, I always recommend summarizing in writing the points that were agreed to each day either at the end of each negotiating session or the next day before negotiations resume. If the other side seems to be backsliding on what you thought was covered, then refer to those written points and try to reach a resolution before moving forward again.

The Indonesians are also similar to the Chinese in their manner of negotiating, particularly as compared to the Japanese. While negotiating is a means to an end for the Japanese, the Indonesians view negotiating (as long as it is not too personal or confrontational) as a fun exercise. There is a long history of bargaining in that part of the world, so negotiations may be extended longer than foreign parties may think is necessary. Relax, and do not push too hard or fast. Giving the impression that you are on a time clock will not be well received by Indonesians, who enjoy the process of negotiating as much as the final outcome.

Finally, forget eye contact when you arrive in Indonesia. Do not try to stare down an Indonesian in a personal situation or during a business negotiation. Staring directly at someone is viewed as rude, boorish, or worse. Remember, being civil, soft-spoken, and nonconfrontational can go a long way toward creating a proper relationship. As in much of Asia, try to get your host or counterpart into a social situation where you can both relax. Avoid prying into family matters, which again would be viewed as inappropriate.

In short, Indonesia is a country with massive natural resources and great prospects for the future. Ignoring the potential for business opportunities in Indonesia is a mistake that any ambitious international company should not make.

CHAPTER ELEVEN

THAILAND VERSUS MALAYSIA: A STUDY IN OPPOSITES

Bangkok is one of the most chaotic and densely populated cities in the world. In the midst of the crowds, traffic jams, and frenetic activity, however, is a sacred temple, a quiet oasis called Wat Phra Kaew. As you climb the steps of the Wat Phra Kaew, better known as the Temple of the Emerald Buddha, you will gaze upon an exquisite Buddha carved out of a massive single block of green jadeite. The overwhelming sense of calm and peace you experience here is a stark contrast to the increasingly industrialized country that Thailand has become.

Thailand

Thailand is one of the most stunningly beautiful places on earth. From its beaches in the south to the hectic Bangkok streets to the lush North, Thailand truly has something for everyone. Thousands of multicolored *wats* (temples) devoted to Buddha dot the countryside as elephants roam in the cool highlands of Chang Mai.

The population of Thailand is three times that of its southern neighbor, Malaysia. Thailand, which was once totally agricultural, has become increasingly industrialized over the last twenty years. Much of the capital that funded Thailand's economic growth is a direct result of foreign direct investment. Although Malaysia is predominantly Muslim, 95 percent of Thais are Buddhists. Most of the small number of Muslims living in Thailand are located in the south, where the two countries border each other.

Ethnicity in Thailand

I have found on each of my trips to Thailand that the Thai people are reserved, respectful of others, and genuinely open to foreign visitors. They are extremely congenial in both business and social situations.

I have observed a unique phenomenon in Thailand that you rarely encounter anywhere else in Southeast Asia. If you hop in a cab at Kuala Lumpur's airport and ask the driver about himself, he will probably remark that he (or she) is Chinese, Malay, or Indian—not necessarily Malaysian. It is common for people in Asia to identify themselves first from their ethnic roots and then from a national perspective. Over the centuries, the Chinese have traveled to the south and Indians have tended to migrate east, following the trade routes throughout what is today's Southeast Asia. Due to these continuing migration patterns, the cab driver may identify himself as Indian or Chinese when he was actually raised in Malaysia, Indonesia, or another Southeast Asia country.

Such self-designation regarding ethnicity is *not* the case in Thailand. The people in northern Thailand, near Chang Mai and Chang Rei, may appear more Chinese in their features than do those who live further south and resemble the descendants of Indians or the indigenous people. However, north, south, east, or west, when you ask someone in Thailand about himself or herself, they will in all likelihood reply, "I am Thai." I have never encountered anyone in Thailand saying he or she is ethnically Chinese or Indian. This is a reflection of how proud the Thai people are about their country and their unique culture.

Social interaction in Thailand is greatly influenced by the Buddhist culture. When meeting someone in Thailand for the first time, you should not immediately extend your hand. It is better to put your hands together as if in prayer and bow slightly. This is what is called the *wa*, and it is how people, whether strangers or friends, greet each other in Thailand. It would be considered impolite or even boorish to use the Western style, look-them-in-the-eye, handshake greeting.

My favorite phrase in Thailand is *mai pen rai*. It is essentially a way of saying, "Whatever you want, that's fine." This phrase acknowledges acceptance even for things that cannot be changed. Most Thais smile and accept whatever comes with grace, as if "bending like a reed in a windstorm." In Thailand you will rarely run into the aggressive in-your-face pushback that is so common elsewhere in Asia. This should not be surprising in a country that is so overwhelmingly Buddhist. Buddhism as a religion advocates a set of philosophical beliefs that support a collaborative as opposed to an individualistic view of one's place in society.

The Thai Government, Military, and the Royal Family

If you visit Thailand even for only a few days, one thing is certain to come up in conversation. Thais will very proudly inform you (assuming you have inquired about their country) that Thailand as a nation has never been conquered by any other people in its long history. While this is not exactly correct, Thailand was never fully colonized like Singapore, Malaysia, and the Philippines. Although Thailand has at certain stages in its history reached political accommodations with its neighbors, this pride of independence is a common trait running through all Thai people.

Thailand's governmental structure is quite unique. The country is a constitutional monarchy since the absolute monarchy was abolished in 1932; however, the current King has greater power and influence over his country than perhaps any king or queen anywhere else in the world. The current head of the monarchy in Thailand, King Bhumibol Adulyadej (also known as Rama IX), has ruled Thailand for more than sixty years. No monarch has ever been on the throne longer than the current King.

As a ruler, King Bhumibol has truly been a wonderful role model for the people of Thailand. The King and his wife (Her Majesty Queen Regent Sirikit) have devoted their lives to improving the lifestyles and livelihood of Thais throughout their country. What most outsiders fail to fully appreciate is that most of the Thai people regard King Bhumibol as a deity. For this reason, any actions of the King are viewed with great respect, and he has thus been able to exercise political power from time to time when necessary.

Foreigners likewise have to be very respectful and should never discuss the Royal Family members in any way. The Thais have a lèse-majesté law (meaning "injury to the majesty"), which makes it a crime for anyone—Thai or otherwise—to offend the monarchy.

It is a vaguely worded law that says, "Whoever defames, insults or threatens the King, the Queen, or the heir to the throne, or the regent" can be found guilty, and jail terms of up to fifteen years are possible. In 2009 a Thai blogger was jailed without bail for posting on the Internet what were viewed as questionable materials about the Royal Family, and there are other such cases pending in Thai courts. The only thing needed to initiate a criminal complaint under this law is for a citizen to report to the police that they think someone has violated the law by insulting a member of the Royal Family. The Thai police will investigate any and all complaints.

The lèse-majesté law has at times had unanticipated consequences. In the early 1950s Richard Rogers and Oscar Hammerstein II penned the famous musical *The King and I*, which was later made into a movie. The original production was a fictional depiction of a former King of Siam (Thailand) called Monkut. Monkut was a predecessor to the current King Bhumibol. In *The King and I*, the king was portrayed as childlike and unsophisticated, which the Thais considered egregiously offensive. Even sixty years later, the play is not a topic that can or should be discussed in Thailand. Needless to say, you won't find a stage production or DVD of *The King and I* in your travels through Thailand. Remember, the King and the Royal Family are considered deities by most Thais.

Over the years, there has been constant tension between the Thai military and the civilian government. Thailand has experienced periodic coups d´état in which members of the military overthrew what they viewed as unpopular or dangerous elected politicians. In 1997, Thailand adopted a constitution that set up a very large legislative body. Its Senate is twice the size of the U.S. Senate, and its House of Representatives is larger than America's Congress. All of these officials were directly elected. In 2006, the then head of the Thai government was Thaksin Shinawatra. A coup d´état occurred in which the military took over the Thai government and appointed its own legislature. Thaksin Shinawatra now lives in exile outside of Thailand and can never return, under threat of being arrested. Since then, Thailand has been in economic and political turmoil with ongoing battles being waged between political activists and the current government. At this point, it is unclear as to when Thailand will return to a truly constitutional form of government.

For all of these reasons, you are strongly advised never to discuss or volunteer your opinion on politics, the Royal Family, prospects for future democracy, or the role of the military in Thailand. It could get you and your company into serious trouble.

Foreign Direct Investment in Thailand

As mentioned earlier, the Thais are a proud people who have technically never been colonized. Because of this fiercely independent tendency, the Thai government has a history of being particularly careful when evaluating the advisability of potential foreign direct investments. Thailand from an early point has been a leader in Southeast Asia in establishing laws and regulations that encourage "domestic content" in manufactured goods made in Thailand. This is one reason why, over the years, foreign automobile companies that sold their vehicles throughout Southeast Asia often chose to establish manufacturing plants in Thailand as opposed to elsewhere. Thai law required that a certain percentage of content be of Thai origin, otherwise the cars could not be sold in Thailand.

The Thai Ministry of Commerce through its Department of Business Development regulates inbound investment in Thailand. In most cases, a foreign company must obtain a validated license under the Foreign Business Act (FBA) in order to conduct business in Thailand. As in other countries, some business sectors are prohibited while others are encouraged. It basically depends on what the Thai government considers strategic and important to its future growth.

Thailand has been quite inventive in understanding the importance of incentivizing certain types of investment. That is why its Board of Investment (BOI) works with local and regional governmental bodies to promote foreign investments that strengthen technologies in Thailand as well as its manufacturing capabilities. If a company has the type of business the Thais are genuinely interested in encouraging, it may find direct and indirect government-sponsored programs that will help underwrite the investment. This is a complicated area requiring close attention. As for joint ventures, partners may discover that in order to be approved by the Board of Investment, they will be encouraged to allow Thai nationals to control a majority interest in the venture (though this does not necessarily apply to a manufacturing venture, which primarily targets the export market). In short, careful planning is required before contemplating a significant equity investment in Thailand. Like the Chinese, the Thais understand the importance of encouraging investment, and not just in the traditional areas surrounding the ports in Bangkok. For this reason, if you are willing to locate your activities outside of the more developed industrial areas, you may find that greater financial and tax incentives are available. Again, as recommended numerous times elsewhere in the book, you need to find the right lawyer in Thailand with whom you can work closely to get the best legal advice and to gain an understanding of the intricacies of doing business within the bureaucracy of Thailand.

Intellectual Property Protection in Thailand

At one time, intellectual property protection in Thailand was almost nonexistent. As foreign investment increased over the last twenty years, the Thai government began to recognize the importance of protecting intellectual property that was owned not only by foreigners but also by Thais themselves. In response to international pressure to protect intellectual property, the Thais set up a specialty tribunal called the Central Intellectual Property and International Trade Court. This specialized court is charged with ensuring that intellectual property laws are enforced regardless of who ultimately owns the intellectual property. Overall, while intellectual property protection in Thailand is not yet up to the standards of countries like Japan or Singapore, my view is that it is improving over time.

MALAYSIA

Malaysia was not independent until 1963, following more than a century as a far-flung colony of the British Empire. It was actually the Japanese invasion during World War II that dealt a death blow to the former British colony, as the British were forced to retreat. Turbulent decades then followed between Malaysian nationalists and the British up to the time of independence.

Following its independence in 1963, Malaysia found itself impoverished with no real infrastructure, but it was a small country with large ambitions. Even with a population of less than 30 million people, it developed over the next twenty years into a very strong player as one of the "Asian Tigers."

How Malaysia became a budding financial and manufacturing center is a remarkable story. Much of it was driven by the former Prime Minister Matahir Mohammed, who interestingly had his training as a medical doctor. It was largely Matahir's vision that forced Malaysia to become an industrialized country very rapidly. If you are walking the streets of Kuala Lumpur and look up, you will see the dual Petronas Towers lighting up the skyline as the most public affirmation that Malaysia has arrived as an economic power. The Petronas Towers are just one example of the expansive ambitions of the former prime minister, many of which were fulfilled during his long tenure. While Malaysia's per capita income is about one-third of its neighbor Singapore, Malaysia is still a strong and important player in Southeast Asia.

Malaysians versus Chinese versus Indians

When Malaysia was officially formed in 1963, Singapore was a small geographic piece of the new nation. A two-year rocky relationship followed between the ethnic Chinese and the ethnic Malays. The end result was Singapore being ejected from Malaysia and declaring its own independence as a country populated primarily by ethnic Chinese.

Historically, the Chinese as a group were perceived as being more successful economically, which was one reason Singapore was expelled and many of the ethnic Chinese then living in Malaysia were encouraged to relocate to the new nation of Singapore. While some conflicts remain, much of that is in the past, but these long-ago events mirror the relationship between ethnic groups in today's

Malaysia. About 55 percent are ethnic Malay, 25 percent Chinese, and about 8 percent Indian. The Malays are predominantly Muslims, and the Chinese and Indians are not. There is also a sizable minority group called the Bumiputras.

It is significant to emphasize that although more than 60 percent of the population practices the Islamic religion, the constitution of Malaysia permits religious freedom. This is important because most of the ethnic Indian population are Hindus, and the ethnic Chinese are primarily Buddhists. My advice when doing business in Malaysia is to look carefully at both the company you are doing business with and the ethnic makeup of its principal owners and/or shareholders. For example, if you are dealing with a company that is owned or controlled by ethnic Chinese Malaysians, the dynamics will be different from those operated by the Bumiputras or Malays. This is why I strongly recommend identifying good local advisors at the beginning of any venture who can help you understand the unique ethnic dynamics of doing business in Malaysia.

Investing in Malaysia

Potential foreign investors looking to Malaysia are best advised to carefully analyze in advance the Malaysian government's current view of regulation. A government-backed social policy in Malaysia in the past required that Malaysians (Bumiputras) must hold at least a 30 percent shareholding in a company. The theory was that major multinational corporations and foreign interests should not be able to invest and hold 100 percent stakes in companies in Malaysia. This policy was designed to protect against what Malaysians view as too much power in the hands of foreign multinationals. That approach was recently radically revised.

Malaysia once had what was known as the Foreign Investment Committee (FIC), which had broad powers to oversee mergers, acquisitions, and inbound investments, and administered a complex set of regulations (FIC Guidelines) that investors had to follow. The FIC and its wide-ranging FIC Guidelines were abolished in June 2009. The goal is now to attract more foreign investment to

Malaysia. It is likely this approach will bring additional investments, which until recently often went to its neighbors (like Singapore).

There are some sectors in Malaysia's economy where the government aggressively encourages inbound investment. For example, the Malaysian government has invested billions in what is called the Multimedia Supercorridor (MSC). The MSC is one of those macro-infrastructure projects heavily supported and subsidized by the central government. The hope behind the MSC is to jump-start Malaysia as a center for research and development and innovation in emerging technology disciplines. To encourage this, a foreign company may be able to set up an operation in Malaysia under the umbrella of the MSC without local partnering. Again, this is still regulated and needs to be carefully reviewed in advance of any investment decision.

It is essential for any company considering doing business in Malaysia to consult with knowledgeable legal counsel. Most (but not all) of the commercially knowledgeable law firms that are familiar with the needs of multinational companies are located in the capital city of Kuala Lumpur. Lawyers you will encounter in Malaysia were educated in Malaysia as well as in the United Kingdom and elsewhere. English in Malaysia is widely used in commercial projects, so do not be unnecessarily concerned about language barriers. With careful planning, you will be able to deal effectively with your Malaysian counterparts.

The Growing Importance of Islamic Finance

Initially it is a challenge for Western-trained lawyers to fully comprehend the concepts of Islamic finance. The reason is that the philosophy and approach of Islamic finance is in some ways the antithesis of capitalism, which had its roots in the West, and socialism, which traditionally had its roots elsewhere.

By way of background, the concepts of Islamic finance gained much wider attention and acceptance following the end of World War II. It was around that time that former colonies of Western countries (such as England and the Netherlands) throughout Asia became independent. Malaysia is an example of this sentiment, because prior to Malaysia becoming an independent nation, Islamic ideas were suppressed. Independence in Malaysia caused a resurgence in interest in the philosophy underlying the principle of Islamic finance.

If you are going to do business in Malaysia, you will need to become at least minimally knowledgeable about the general concepts of Islamic finance. Islamic finance is intended to embody the precepts of Islamic law (Shari'a) by creating and making Shari'a-compliant financial services available to a potential market of over 1.3 billion Muslims around the world. No one knows for sure the current size of the market, but some observers estimate that about $700 billion in assets now under management are Shari'a compliant. This potential market in the future is projected at $4 trillion USD. Understanding this opportunity, Malaysia is working hard to become the top center for Islamic finance in Asia.

The basis of Islamic finance comes from the Qur'an, which sets forth the fundamental teachings of Islam. Under the Qur'an, two things are prohibited related to finance. First, it is against the teaching of the Islamic religion for interest to be paid on loans. Instead, the philosophy is that profits and losses are to be communally shared in such a way as to avoid going against the teachings of the Qur'an. There is a term, *riba*, that is a prohibition against usury. *Riba* does not mean usury in a Western sense, but rather applies to any interest that might be charged on loans, and it is prohibited. Second, any financial activities engaged in by Muslims must be socially responsible.

In terms of Western banking, the conventional way of doing business is for an individual or company to pay interest on money it borrows from a financial institution. However, since an interest-focused system is rejected under the Qur'an, the Islamic approach to banking is more asset based. Because different financial structures exist in Islamic finance, there are business terms that describe specific transactions that are permitted under the Qur'an and current interpretations. Examples of these specialized terms are *mudarabah*, *hibah*, *ijarah*, *musharakah*, *takaful*, *musawamah*, and *murabahah*.

Murabahah is a type of secured lending transaction that in its simplest terms refers to a customer who wants to buy property but needs to be able to finance the transaction. This is often used with the sales and purchases of a commodity. Under Islamic finance concepts, the buyer cannot borrow money or pay interest in order to purchase the property. Instead, under *murabahah*, the bank itself first buys the property in question for its own account from a third party. Then the customer agrees to acquire that asset on credit, which reflects a marked-up price. At that point, the bank can sell the product to the customer, and the transaction, if structured properly, should be Shari'a compliant.

Ijarah is structured differently in that a lease exists until such a time as the purchaser actually owns or uses the property. In theory, the bank is providing use of a service or assets for a set fee. To do this, a bank sets up a special-purpose vehicle (SPV). Because the bank knows from its discussions with its customer that the customer actually wants to acquire the property, the SPV purchases the property and holds title to the property. The customer then agrees to make monthly payments against the value of the lease to acquire the property. These payments by a customer are amortized much like normal bank loans in the West. Again, due to the structure, the transaction can go forward without the actual payment of interest on the lease.

Takaful is the approach taken to insurance as used in the Islamic financial sector. Obviously, protection from risk is something every businessperson needs to address. The theory is that individuals should share risks by purchasing policies and pooling resources. Here, a "for profit" insurance venture would be prohibited, but one in which parties took care of each others' needs can, if structured appropriately, be Shari'a compliant.

In short, Islamic finance is a complex area of the law in which you will need to seek advice from competent legal professionals, many of whom practice in Malaysia. Without an understanding of the principles of Islamic finance, the foreign investor is likely to encounter confusion and challenges when negotiating and structuring deals in Malaysia.

The Malaysian Governmental System

Like Thailand, its neighbor to the north, Malaysia has a hybrid political system. There are various states within Malaysia that have hereditary rulers. These rulers hold more ceremonial positions than actual power, but they can still exercise political influence within the country.

The real governing in Malaysia is done by the prime minister (and his cabinet) who, like in the United Kingdom, ascends to power as a member of the Parliament. The Malaysian Parliament is seated in Kuala Lumpur. If you understand how the British system works, you will see great similarities between that and Malaysia. Local legislative bodies exist in each state of Malaysia; however, most of the important policy decisions are made at the federal level in the Malaysian Parliament.

The most dominant political party in Malaysia is the United Malays National Organization (UMNO), which has essentially controlled Malaysia since it declared its independence. To better understand Malaysia, it is important to work with local advisors who can speak to any of the myriad of political issues that can and will affect foreign investors.

Resolution of Commercial Disputes

Legal counsel representing or working with a foreign investor in Malaysia needs to think about dispute resolution. Both local courts and arbitration are options. My recommendation is that you first consider opting for commercial arbitration as opposed to local courts. There are a variety of reasons for this, such as confidentiality, flexibility in rules, and how arbitration is conducted. Also, if a dispute involving your company is time sensitive, arbitration is probably the way to go.

In Kuala Lumpur, there is a Regional Centre for Arbitration (KLRCA). Formed in 1978, it is supported by the Malaysian government, though not officially a part of the government. The KLRCA has a website (www.rcakl.org.my) that fully describes its rules, fees, and other services. Also, I have seen foreign investors who deal with

Malaysian companies elect to hold commercial arbitrations in Singapore since the Singapore International Arbitration Centre (SIAC) is very close by, and some foreign companies view Singapore as a neutral venue to resolve commercial disputes.

CHAPTER TWELVE

VIETNAM AND THE OTHER PLAYERS

The image of the final helicopter lifting off of the roof of the U.S. Embassy in Saigon on April 28, 1975, is seared into the memories of many Americans. Two days later, all American forces withdrew from Saigon, which was later renamed Ho Chi Minh City. This somber moment marked the end of the Vietnam War and the absolute low point of U.S.–Vietnam relations.

The Vietnam of 1975 no longer exists. Today, Vietnam has its arms open to welcome foreign—and American—investment in its economy.

VIETNAM

Why Vietnam? Why Now?

Over the last four decades, products manufactured in Asia have followed a daisy chain of countries as manufacturers have sought to find the lowest-cost labor venues. During the 1960s, Japan was a rising manufacturing star, but the label "Made in Japan" back then was not a sign of quality; instead it signified cheaply made goods. Japan's poor reputation for quality was swiftly supplanted by Korea as Japan moved up the scale of manufacturing sophistication. Taiwan subsequently became the next home of inexpensive goods, followed by the "Tigers" of Southeast Asia, including Indonesia, Malaysia, Thailand, the Philippines, and Singapore. Most of these countries staked out their reputations in global markets as members of the Association of Southeast Asia Nations (ASEAN), in which they not only exported what they made but also traded goods among themselves. Twenty years ago, China, with its excellent infrastructure and very low labor rates, became the world's new manufacturing center.

"Why Vietnam? Why Now?" reflects today's fact that China is no longer the lowest-cost manufacturing center in Asia. Manufacturing in China is now too expensive for some companies. For those companies seeking to produce goods which require a high labor content but are not particularly sophisticated, Vietnam is the new kid on the block. Vietnam today looks a lot like China did twenty-five years ago, but whether Vietnam will become as highly successful as China in manufacturing remains to be seen.

Five Factors for Considering Vietnam as a Place to Do Business

Factor One

Vietnam is a developing country in the most classic sense. For example, it is more subject to inflationary pressures than are more developed countries. Doing business in Vietnam requires a great deal of patience because the overall country lags behind its peers in many ways. Nevertheless, Vietnam's developing status is one of the key reasons it can provide a large, inexpensive labor pool to manufacturers.

Factor Two

The Vietnamese legal system is notably underdeveloped. The country's laws and regulations are constantly changing, which presents a major challenge to foreign investors, particularly larger multinational corporations. It is difficult to predict with any accuracy how an investment in Vietnam will be treated by the government in the future, which makes planning tricky when a foreign company is contemplating a project that requires significant capital investment.

Factor Three

Vietnam's infrastructure is significantly underdeveloped, as was China's twenty-five years ago. Manufacturers who want to move their goods efficiently from the factory floor to a port in Vietnam and then ship them out to export markets will encounter constant challenges. In addition to its ports, Vietnam's power and transportation systems are weak. Another continuing problem throughout

Vietnam is flooding, which occurs periodically even in the major cities because of the country's low lying geography. Consequently, foreign companies that plan to set up manufacturing operations in Vietnam or have subcontracts there must be sure their factories are sited in places that are not prone to flooding.

Factor Four

The Vietnamese government actively wants to encourage inbound investment because it sees how foreign investment led to the development of China and other countries throughout Asia. Nevertheless, the bureaucratic structure in Vietnam is quite convoluted. Foreign investors need to work deftly not just on a national basis but also with local government officials. Local regional areas can offer attractive tax incentives to do business in their jurisdictions, but investors must be certain that any promised financial incentives are real.

Factor Five

Actually getting approved to do business in Vietnam takes time and is governed by a rigid set of regulations. A myriad of business approvals and licenses are required before a company can begin operations. You should never actually start conducting your business activities in Vietnam without obtaining all the required documentation in advance. Never rely on oral representations that your project will have "no problems." Failure to strictly comply with the provisions of government-issued licenses can in fact result in serious problems. Finally, because so many approvals and licenses are required, you may find the cost of setting up a business in Vietnam is high, at least initially, as opposed to other places such as China, Taiwan, or even Japan.

Expatriate Workers in Vietnam

Just as inbound foreign investment is highly regulated in Vietnam, the same is true for expatriate workers. Most expatriates who come to Vietnam for employment will be required to obtain a work permit (though there are some exceptions). The approval process will require proof that the expatriate has real specific skills or is to hold a high managerial position. The Vietnamese government goal is to ultimately have Vietnam nationals fill these positions, although it is understood that some executive positions must be filled by expatriates. However, you should expect that with any size company there will be a government-imposed limit on the number of expatriates who will be approved to work in Vietnam.

Intellectual Property in Vietnam

Much like China twenty-five years ago, Vietnam does have intellectual property (IP) laws, but they are quite basic. Foreign companies face a constant challenge striving to protect their intellectual property rights in Vietnam. To date, anticounterfeiting efforts by the government have not been particularly effective. Protection of trademarks remains an area where owners must be very watchful.

It is important to note that intellectual property laws in Vietnam do not discriminate just against foreign investors, but are a reflection of how they are viewed generally within Vietnam's society. In the long run, Vietnam's IP laws should improve with time, as has happened in other countries, but as a developing country such protection is a work in process.

The Delicate Art of Negotiating in Vietnam

Before you go to Vietnam for the first time, you should research both its business practices and etiquette. There are a wide variety of resource materials that will help you get a better feel for negotiating in Vietnam.

There are a few basic points that will assist during the process. First, as in China, *face* is extremely important in Vietnam. The Vietnamese are polite and not outwardly aggressive, so modesty is a good tactic to adopt. Never brag about the size of your company or your background and experience to the Vietnamese.

When you seek to cultivate contacts in Vietnam, you have two options. The first option is to work with a company that has experience dealing in Vietnam on behalf of foreign investors. Some of these companies are good; others are less effective. The second option is to ask someone you know to introduce you to a potential Vietnamese contact. Try to have a written introduction sent to a possible contact with adequate advance notice so they can prepare. You can generally assume that you will need to use an interpreter in Vietnam, because most businesspeople do not speak English. Government officials will also expect you to use an interpreter when you interact with them.

Although forming a relationship is always important, Vietnamese officials are typically more anxious to get down to business than is the case elsewhere in Asia. These officials are highly sought after, so you can immediately begin talking business in a meeting after exchanging cards (with English on one side and Vietnamese on the other). As described earlier, the licensing and permitting process in Vietnam can be quite time consuming. While the Vietnamese are trying to shorten the period, you will need to devote significant time and resources in order to make sure everything is in place.

Unfortunately for foreign businesswomen, it will be more difficult to do business in Vietnam than in other countries such as China. This cultural reality may not exist everywhere in Asia, but it is quite real in Vietnam.

Finally, because of the type of government that exists in Vietnam, you should assume that private communications will be seen or heard by others, including telephone conversations and documents received via fax at a hotel. Many foreign investors fail to anticipate the need to take such precautions and run the risk of inadvertently disclosing protected information.

Bangladesh

Bangladesh, a large country in terms of both population and size, is not well known outside of Asia. Unfortunately, the publicity Bangladesh typically receives is as a result of violent typhoons and flooding that regularly beset the country. Bangladesh sits at the confluence of three of the world's great major river systems, including the Ganges. Its landscape is essentially an immense delta with rich soil, making Bangladesh a country that remains largely agricultural.

While the official language of Bangladesh is Bengali, English is widely used in business. Islam is the state religion in Bangladesh, but other religions are accepted and freely practiced.

In recent years, Bangladesh has attracted the interest of foreign investors for several reasons. First, the country has very low-cost labor. The top market for its exports is the United States, and the major export industry coming out of Bangladesh is clothing (garments). Although Bangladesh is a poor country, its annual growth over the last twenty years exceeded 5 percent. It imports a wide variety of manufactured products and equipment and exports clothing, fish, and agricultural products such as rice and tea. A major source of income for Bangladesh is its overseas workforce, which repatriates significant funds back into the country to family members. The major challenge Bangladesh faces across the board is its significantly underdeveloped infrastructure. One bright spot for Bangladesh is its as yet untapped natural gas reserves, which should provide additional income in the coming years.

CAMBODIA—THE KINGDOM OF CAMBODIA

Cambodia is a constitutional monarchy with a parliament. As an underdeveloped country with tourism as one of its major income producers, each year Cambodia hosts visitors from around the world who come to see the breathtaking grounds and temples of Angkor Wat and hundreds of other significant archaeological sites throughout the country. Cambodia has a long and proud Buddhist tradition, which is reflected in its people.

Cambodia remains primarily an agricultural country and is a major producer of rice for both domestic and international markets. Nevertheless, Cambodia has an emerging garment industry, similar to Bangladesh. In recent years, the Cambodian government has begun to devote scarce resources to developing the country's infrastructure, particularly its roads and railroads. While Cambodia's infrastructure is still not up to world standards, there is some hope for improvement. Recently oil and gas reserves were discovered off the coast of Cambodia. You can bet these reserves will be exploited over the next several years as they promise to produce new revenue streams for the government.

Laos—The Lao People's Democratic Republic

Laos, one of the least developed countries in Asia, is a member of ASEAN. It is a single-party socialist country that has made foreign direct investment an ongoing challenge for decades. The few goods produced in Laos are traded with its most immediate neighbors (China, Thailand, and Vietnam). The major problem Laos faces is that it basically has no infrastructure other than its extensive river system. Laos currently imports all of its oil and gas, but does export some of its locally produced hydroelectric energy power to its neighbors Vietnam and Thailand. Because Laos has deposits of gold, coal, tin, copper, and bauxite, it has the potential for investment. However, until Laos addresses the infrastructure needed to exploit its resources, the country is not likely to be a major target of inbound foreign investment.

Brunei—The State of Brunei Darussalam

Brunei is a former colony of Britain that gained its independence in 1984. Located on the island of Borneo, Brunei is a newly industrialized country. In fact, it ranks fourth in the world by size of gross domestic product (GDP) per capita, as determined by purchasing power parity. The key explanation for the success of Brunei is its massive oil and natural gas reserves, which account for more than half of its GDP. The majority of Brunei's exports are energy related. Brunei maintains close relationships with most countries in the region, particularly Singapore and the Philippines. Two-thirds of its population belongs to the Islamic faith. Brunei is a Shari'a country, and as a result certain things are carefully controlled by government officials. For example, alcohol is prohibited in Brunei except for limited use by expatriates. Brunei's greatest achievement since achieving its independence was to significantly develop its infrastructure.

Burma—Union of Myanmar

For almost fifty years, the military has controlled the government of Burma and effectively suppressed all potential democratic movements. As this book is being written, the U.S. government has a comprehensive embargo against all commercial activities involving Burma. The Office of Foreign Assets Control of the U.S. Department of Treasury strictly enforces the embargo regulations, and violating the embargo can carry serious civil and sometimes criminal penalties, as specified in the regulations in Executive Order No. 13047 issued by President Clinton on May 20, 1997. In short, the embargo prohibits investments in Burma by any U.S. person or entity as defined in the regulations. The regulations also prohibit importation into the United States of any products produced in Burma. Any U.S. company or its joint venture partners, employees, or agents should carefully consult the regulations before considering doing any kind of business in Burma.

NEPAL—THE FEDERAL DEMOCRATIC REPUBLIC OF NEPAL

Nepal is one of the poorest countries in the world. Three-quarters of its economy is agricultural, and most of what is produced is at subsistence levels. One of the few foreign currency earners for Nepal is tourism. Therefore, unless a company is somehow involved in the tourism industry, it is unlikely that Nepal will be a target for foreign direct investment activities.

BHUTAN—THE KINGDOM OF BHUTAN

Once a British Crown colony, Bhutan is a now constitutional monarchy. In 2008, Bhutan approved a new constitution that changed the status of the traditional monarchy. Under the constitution, the National Assembly was granted the authority to remove the monarchy if the legislators vote by a supermajority to do so.

Like Nepal, Bhutan is an extremely poor country with subsistence agriculture. When this book was being written, there were no existing formal diplomatic relations between the United States and Bhutan. Where contacts are needed, the U.S. Embassy in New Delhi is the place to go in order to open a line of communication with the government of Bhutan. Unless you have a very unique and specific business opportunity, it is unlikely that Bhutan is a target for foreign investment.

THE INDEPENDENT STATE OF PAPUA NEW GUINEA

This island nation in the Pacific has less than 7 million population, of which more than 80% live in rural environments. It is extremely poor, with subsistence agricultural products the mainstay of the economy. There are few economic opportunities here to attract foreign investors.

The Democratic Socialist Republic of Sri Lanka

Sri Lanka is an island nation located off the southern tip of India in the Indian Ocean. As with its neighbor to the north, the British East India Company transformed this small country into a British crown colony in the early 19th century. Probably best known around the world as Ceylon, the name was changed to Sri Lanka in the early 1970s. For more than 40 years, the country endured bloody and intense armed conflicts between the minority Tamils and the majority Sinhalese, and it was only in 2009 that the government declared a formalized end to this civil war. The form of government of Sri Lanka is a parliamentary system with a president who is popularly elected for a six-year term. Sri Lanka remains an economy heavily dependent upon agriculture, though it also has a measurable presence in the clothing and textiles industries. Sri Lanka has found itself vulnerable whenever the world economy experienced a downtown, as it did in 2008-09. Foreign investors should identify a targeted project or area of interest before pursuing significant investments in Sri Lanka.

CHAPTER THIRTEEN
GETTING READY TO GO

It was a dream come true for the young lawyer. On his very first visit to Asia, he found himself in Osaka, Japan, on a trip sponsored by the U.S. State Department, preparing to speak before a large gathering of high-level Japanese businessmen and government officials. The evening before his speech, the lawyer was the guest of honor at a traditional Japanese restaurant, an experience for which he had done some advance research. He had diligently practiced using chopsticks and knew to remove his shoes and wear the slippers provided so as not to damage the delicate straw tatami mats covering the floor. The young lawyer felt very confident and was prepared to dazzle his Japanese hosts with an encyclopedic knowledge of trade issues and intellectual property.

When asked whether he would prefer a Japanese or a Western menu, the lawyer replied "Japanese, of course. I love Japanese food. I eat it all the time." However, this was a bit of an exaggeration, since the lawyer had only once eaten sukiyaki. "Then we will begin with sushi," announced his hosts. Not sure what exactly sushi was, the young lawyer sipped his green tea and tried to watch his hosts for clues but, being proper Japanese, they waited until he, the guest of honor, began to eat. The lawyer picked up his chopsticks and looked down at his plate. Not quite sure what to do with the slices of raw fish lying on what appeared to be a rice stick, he looked for something a bit easier to start with. He spotted a mound of greenish substance shaped like a small pyramid. It looked innocuous enough, so he popped the green pyramid into his mouth with a smile. It went down easily enough, but the lawyer soon felt a burning sensation swell in his throat, sweat broke out on his forehead, and he felt as if he was having a heart attack.

His Japanese hosts began to laugh uncontrollably and handed the struggling lawyer one glass of Sapporo beer after another until the burning in his stomach slowly began to subside. That young lawyer, who thought himself so worldly, had mistakenly downed in a single gulp a full portion of wasabi, the unique and fiery Japanese radish. The Japanese hosts could not stop laughing as the American sat in abject misery. Any semblance of his pride was gone—he had completely lost face in front of his hosts and himself.

This story took place twenty-five years ago, and I was the young lawyer wallowing in physical pain and total embarrassment. Since then I have visited fifty countries on countless business trips attempting to keep my clients (and myself) out of trouble. I confess that I have made many mistakes over the years, but I have also learned a great deal about international law and business, particularly in Asia where the majority of my time has been spent. I wrote this book to help others navigate between Western ways of conducting business and the diverse Asian perspectives. The chapters are filled with practical insights; and the anecdotes I included reflect real-life experiences. While my target audience is lawyers, consider sharing the ideas in this book with your colleagues because most of the concepts should interest businesspeople as well.

THE THREE-STEP PLAN

While this book can help you develop a fundamental understanding of doing business throughout Asia, you will have to go further if you are really serious about putting these ideas into practice. Just reading a chapter of this book is a bit like relying on a CliffsNotes version of *Hamlet* for an English literature class—you will get the major plot points and character names, but the beauty and nuances of the original work are likely to pass you by.

In order to prepare for negotiations overseas, I recommend an approach that I have followed consistently over the years. To begin, it is a universal truth that every country's past greatly influences how it functions today, and this truism is particularly important in Asia. Before visiting any country for the first time, I follow what I call the Three-Step Plan. My Three-Step Plan focuses on analyzing the following factors:

- The country's historical relationship with its neighbors
- How its economy functions
- The way political institutions and politics influence the government's economic and social conduct

Step One: Appreciating the Importance of Historical Events

Most of us will probably agree that historical events have a major impact upon how a country conducts itself. Nevertheless, I have often observed businesspeople ignoring how important history is in influencing present-day dealings, particularly in Asia. For example, how could anyone appreciate the depth and complexity of the conflict between the Israelites and their neighbors in the Middle East without understanding their historical relationship?

The 100-Year Look Back

When analyzing a country's history, begin by looking back over the last hundred years or so. Recent events are the freshest, and in some cases individuals may still be around who have experienced those events. The best example of historical events impacting the present is the conflicted relationship between the Japanese, the Chinese, and the Koreans. With the rise of militarism in Japan in the 1930s, Japan struck out and invaded parts of Manchuria, Mongolia, and then China. Even earlier, the Japanese had annexed without any legitimacy the lands that are currently North and South Korea. The atrocities inflicted by the Japanese militarists on the Koreans and the Chinese during these invasions are well documented. The Chinese vividly remember the "Rape of Nanjing" during World War II, when Japanese soldiers executed anywhere between 100,000 and 200,000 Chinese in a matter of days. After the Korean peninsula was annexed by the Japanese at the beginning of the 20th century, Koreans were allowed to speak only the Japanese language for three decades. Korea's language and most of its rich culture were essentially destroyed, a fact few Westerners appreciate. Given these horrific experiences, it is no surprise that deep wells of resentment toward the Japanese still widely exist throughout China and Korea today. While official government exchanges and dealings among these three significant political powers have improved in recent years, it will take generations for the underlying bitterness to truly disappear. History has a long memory.

This example illustrates why it makes sense for anyone doing business in Asia to go back at least 100 years to learn what major events occurred that might affect future relations. Moreover, there are some issues from recent Asian history that are still so emotionally explosive they cannot be brought up in conversation, such as the shocking example of "comfort women." During World War II, the Japanese military illegally conscripted teenage girls from Korea, China, the Philippines, and elsewhere in Asia and forced them to work as prostitutes in brothels run by the Japanese military. This sad fact has been well documented, and only in recent years has the Japanese government begun to make financial reparations to those comfort women who are still alive. Remember, this recent historical issue and others like it should never be discussed at any point during negotiations or private conversations. If the topic is brought up in your presence, you as a Westerner should simply listen without comment.

The Long Look Back

If you really want to gain an in-depth understanding of a country, you may have to look back several hundred, perhaps several thousand, years. Take China for example. The Chinese civilization dates back more than 4,000 years. When most people in the West were still living in caves and wearing animal skins, China prospered as an advanced and sophisticated civilization. Then for 500 years up until the 1930s, the time of the Revolution of the Communist Party in China, Western powers forcibly dominated the Chinese in many ways that the Chinese remember vividly. The Chinese still resent the British for addicting millions of Chinese to opium during the 19th century solely to make China open up its domestic market to the English and others. One of the reasons you are now seeing a resurgence of nationalism in China is because it has become economically strong and more politically aggressive in reaction to 500 years of Western domination.

Religion

In addition to learning about a country's history, never overlook the dynamics of religion in a society. While in some countries like Japan religion has not been a major factor in influencing business and culture, Malaysia is the opposite. In Malaysia, you will find three major ethnic groups comprising most of the population—the Malays, those of Indian heritage, and the Chinese. Each ethnic group in Malaysia embraces different religious and cultural beliefs, and understanding how these ways of life developed helps greatly in doing business in this diverse country.

In short, learning as much as you can about the history and underlying culture of a country is critical if you hope to accurately predict how its people may or may not react in certain business and social circumstances.

Step Two: How a Country's Economy Functions

Again, before visiting any foreign country, take the time to gain an insight into how that country's economy functions and what factors drive the economy both positively and negatively. China operates a totally controlled central economy in which all major economic decisions are either directly or indirectly approved by the Chinese government (the Chinese Communist Party). While the Chinese domestic market has become more open in recent years, never underestimate the power and influence of the Chinese bureaucracy in governing how it functions. On the other hand, Hong Kong has a wide-open economy—one of the freest anywhere in the world. Hong Kong is a Special Administrative Region (SAR) that is technically part of the People's Republic of China but in reality is still very separate. As long as you pay your minimum business taxes and do not create problems with the PRC authorities on the mainland, almost anything goes in Hong Kong. At least for the next fifty years, Hong Kong should continue to enjoy a freer and more open economy than anywhere else in China. Consequently, many foreign investors (from the United States, Europe, and elsewhere) choose to set up a Hong Kong limited liability company and then conduct their business activities in China through their Hong Kong entity. In contrast, Korea wields a strict hand when evaluating and approving proposed foreign investments. Surprisingly, the Japanese, while quite controlling in the past, have exhibited far less scrutiny over foreign economic investments in recent years.

When structuring a business transaction, the key is to determine what level of control a country's central government is likely to exercise over your activities and in approving, or denying, your right to do business there. For example, Thailand, like some other countries, has passed a "local content law" that requires that set percentages of manufactured goods to be sold in Thailand must be of Thai origin. This is why, years ago, Japanese car companies set up manufacturing in Thailand as opposed to elsewhere in order to comply with local content requirements under Thai law.

Yet another factor for foreign counsel and investors to consider is a country's currency. Japan's yen is a fully convertible international "hard" currency that floats and is traded freely on global financial markets, while India is more circumspect in dealing with the value of its currency (the rupee). Many currencies in Asia were badly damaged during the Asian financial crisis of 1997–1998. At one point in 1998, the ringgit (Malaysia's currency) lost about 50 percent of its value. In response, Malaysia announced that foreign currencies within its borders could not be exported without the central government's permission. For more than a year, foreign companies with non-ringgit currencies in Malaysia found those funds frozen while the financial crisis sorted itself out. Indonesia, which did not adopt Malaysia's approach, saw the rupee devalued more than 80 percent in a matter of weeks.

Step Three: The Influence of Public Institutions and Politics on National Conduct

This book presents numerous examples of the roles that public institutions in Asian countries play with foreign direct investors. In addition, central governments throughout Asia set policies that determine the parts of the economy that will or will not receive preferential financial incentives. Thirty years ago, India and China both had roughly the same size economies. Since then, China succeeded in achieving higher and more sustained annual growth than India because China aggressively funded its own infrastructure projects. These projects over three decades produced tens of thousands of miles of roads, ports, railroads, and massive electrical capacity that were key to China creating a nationwide manufacturing industrial infrastructure. Singapore is another example of a small but very strongly controlled country with extremely powerful public institutions. Singapore also boasts the well-deserved reputation of being one of the least corrupt countries anywhere in the world because Singaporean law holds its public officials to the highest possible ethical standards and strictly enforces these laws. Other Asian countries neither enact nor enforce such high ethical standards for their public officials.

Conclusion

Before you grab your passport and start packing your suitcase, take time to prepare by giving yourself a crash course on the history, economy, politics, and public institutions in each country where you expect to do business. These insights will enable you to negotiate better and make a more fully informed evaluation of whether you should move forward with a deal. When in doubt, smile and admit to your foreign counterparts that while you love their country, you still have much to learn. Say it with conviction and you are halfway there. Be humble and embrace the diversity. The rest is just hard work and a dash of luck. Enjoy the ride. I have.

INDEX